LADY CONSTANCE LYTTON

In Memory of Frank

Forever sleeping in his armchair

23-01-2021

Lady Constance Lytton

Prison Reformer and Suffragette

Abigail Hamilton-Thompson

Pen & Sword HISTORY

AN IMPRINT OF PEN & SWORD BOOKS LTD.
YORKSHIRE – PHILADELPHIA

First published in Great Britain in 2025 by
Pen & Sword History
An imprint of
Pen & Sword Books Ltd
Yorkshire - Philadelphia

Copyright © Abigail Hamilton-Thompson, 2025

ISBN 978 1 52677 503 0

The right of Abigail Hamilton-Thompson to be identified as the Author of this work has been asserted by her in accordance with the Copyright, Designs and Patents Act 1988.

A CIP catalogue record for this book is available from the British Library.

All rights reserved. No part of this book may be reproduced, transmitted, downloaded, decompiled or reverse engineered in any form or by any means, electronic or mechanical including photocopying, recording or by any information storage and retrieval system, without permission from the Publisher in writing. NO AI TRAINING: Without in any way limiting the Author's and Publisher's exclusive rights under copyright, any use of this publication to "train" generative artificial intelligence (AI) technologies to generate text is expressly prohibited. The Author and Publisher reserve all rights to license uses of this work for generative AI training and development of machine learning language models.

Typeset in INDIA by IMPEC eSolutions
Printed and bound in England by CPI Group (UK) Ltd, Croydon, CR0 4YY

The Publisher's authorised representative in the EU for product safety is Authorised Rep Compliance Ltd., Ground Floor, 71 Lower Baggot Street, Dublin D02 P593, Ireland. www.arccompliance.com

For a complete list of Pen & Sword titles please contact:

PEN & SWORD BOOKS LIMITED
George House, Units 12 & 13, Beevor Street,
Off Pontefract Road, Barnsley, S71 1HN, UK
E-mail: enquiries@pen-and-sword.co.uk
Website: www.pen-and-sword.co.uk

or

PEN AND SWORD BOOKS
1950 Lawrence Road, Havertown, PA 19083, USA
E-mail: uspen-and-sword@casematepublishers.com
Website: www.penandswordbooks.com

Contents

Acknowledgements — vi
Dedication to Prisoners — vii

Chapter 1 The Early Years, 1869-1897 — 1

Chapter 2 Relationship with John Ponsonby and Maurice Baring, 1897-1908 — 17

Chapter 3 Becoming a Suffragette, 1908 — 35

Chapter 4 Early Prison Years, 1909 — 55

Chapter 5 Becoming Jane Warton, 1910 — 85

Chapter 6 Declining Health and Stroke, 1910-1914 — 112

Chapter 7 Marie Stopes' Birth Control Clinic Improvements and Con's Final Years, 1914-1923 — 140

Biographical Appendix — 168
Bibliography — 180
Index — 182

Acknowledgements

Thank you to Jill Campbell of Knebworth House Archives for her help with the many letters belonging to Lady Constance Lytton; to the Honorable Henry Lytton-Cobbold for the use of pictures from the Knebworth House Archives; to Beverley Cook from the Museum of London for allowing me to view the items relating to Con; to the librarians of the British Library for their assistance; the librarians at the Women's Library at LSE for their patience; and my thanks also to the archivists of Hertfordshire Archives.

Thank you also to Heather Williams from Pen & Sword for her editing work and to my family for supporting me with this book.

Abigail Hamilton-Thompson, 2025

Author's note

Lady Constance was most commonly referred to as Con or Conny during her short life. To avoid any confusion, I shall therefore refer to her as Con throughout.

Dedication to Prisoners

Constance Lytton *Prisons and Prisoners* (1914)

When, for a short while, I shared your lot, I asked myself through all my waking hours if there were any friendly thought which could act beneficently for all prisoners, no matter how various the training of their previous lives, no matter whether distress of circumstance, drunkenness, selfish action, cruelty, or madness had been the cause which brought them into prison.

And there seemed this one thing. It is a single idea but needs many words to give it shape.

Lay hold of your inward self and keep tight hold. Reverence yourself. Be just, kind and forgiving to yourself. For the inner you of yourself is surely the only means of communication for you with any good influence you may once have enjoyed or hope someday to find, the only window through which you can look upon a happier and more lovable life, the only door through which some day you will be able to escape, unbarring it to your own release from all that is helpless, selfish, and unkind in your present self.

Public opinion, which sent you to prison, and your gaolers, who have to keep you there, are mostly concerned with your failings. Every hour of prison existence will remind you of these afresh. Unless you are able to keep alight within yourself the remembrance of acts and thoughts which were good, a belief in your own power to exist freely when you are once more out of prison, how can any other human being help you? If not the inward power, how can any external power avail?

But if you have this comforter with you, hourly keeping up communication with all that you have known and loved of good in your life, with all the possibilities for good that you know of – in your hands, your mind, your heart – then when you are released from prison, however lonely you may be, or poor, or despised by your neighbours, you will have a friend who can really help you.

There will be people who visit you in prison, and who watch over you at first when you come out. They will try to help you, but unless they truly understand your lot, understanding your goodness as well as your badness, and sympathising with your badness as well as with your goodness, they will seem far off from you. Who knows, though, but what you may help them? In my ignorance and impudence I went into prison hoping to help prisoners. So far as I know, I was unable to do anything for them. But the prisoners helped me. They seemed at times the direct channels between me and God himself, imbued with the most friendly and powerful goodness that I have ever met.

Prisoners, I wish I could give to you, for your joy, something of the help you gave to me, and that in many ways I could follow your example.

Chapter 1

The Early Years, 1869-1897

Lady Constance (Con) Georgina Bulwer-Lytton was born on 12 February 1869 and died on 22 May 1923. As her sister, Lady Betty, later wrote in her book, *Letters of Constance Lytton*, of the fifty-four years she was alive, she only spent four of those doing the public work for which she became so well known.

Con was the third child, and middle daughter, of Robert Bulwer-Lytton and Edith Villiers. The Lyttons were a prominent family but were considered by some to have had a troubled, shameful past. Con's grandfather, the famous novelist Edward Bulwer-Lytton, rebuked his wife Rosina after she rebelled against his infidelities. He later decided to take custody of his children and reduced her to a modest income. After she satirised him in her own novel *Cheveley, or the Man of Honour* (1839), he had her committed to an asylum in 1858. Rosina described the experience in her memoir *A Blighted Life* (1880). During her time there, Rosina Bulwer-Lytton refused to eat, but when told by a superintendent that this refusal would be evidence of her insanity, she began to eat with much gusto. Con's grandfather, Edward Bulwer-Lytton, was an MP and the 1st Baron of Lytton. He was offered the crown of Greece after King Otto abdicated in 1862 but declined. As a novelist, Edward was famous for penning the opening line 'It was a dark and stormy night' in his novel *Paul Clifford* about a highway robber during the French Revolution. He used the pen name Owen Meredith for his poetry, his most popular verse being *Lucile*.

Con's maternal great-grandmother, Anna Wheeler, was also a writer and an advocate of women's rights. She had visited asylums and, like her future great-granddaughter, wanted to make a name for herself in the reformation of prisons. She had worked with the poor and underfed but was forced to leave her Guernsey home in 1816 after channelling £20,000 of the island's finances into poor relief. Both mother and daughter had been born and grew up in Ireland, which likewise faced its own challenges in hunger and starvation in the nineteenth century.

Edward and Rosina's only son, Robert, wanted to become a poet, but his father decided that it would not be proper for 'two of the same name to have a permanent reputation in literature'. Consequently, Robert joined the diplomatic service instead and was a protégé of Benjamin Disraeli in domestic affairs for his work as Viceroy of India, although he did later have some work published.

Born in Vienna on 12 February 1869, Con's childhood consisted of moving from one place to another due to her father's profession as Secretary to the Embassy. First, they moved from Vienna to Paris, then on to Lisbon and when she was 7, the family moved to India, where Robert began a reportedly doomed tenure as Viceroy: in 1877 he proclaimed Queen Victoria to be Empress of India, the Great Famine of 1876-1878 took place, and the second Anglo-Afghan War occurred, with both of the latter events blamed more-or-less on Robert. He had overseen the regular export of grain, thus weakening the cultural and economic strength of Southern India and had also held a great banquet for 60,000 people in honour of Queen Victoria's coronation as Empress, while his diplomatic mission, otherwise seen as an invasion of Kabul, triggered the second Anglo-Afghan War.

The Bulwer-Lytton family at this time epitomised colonialism, aristocracy and wealth. Robert was also rumoured to be a philanderer, having taken up with an American actress. Perhaps Con's later transformation into the 'working-class' Jane Warton was a reaction against this upper-class personification and her desire to sympathise with the poor and oppressed. The Bulwer-Lytton's first-born son,

Edward Rowland John, died at the age of 6 in 1871. Another boy, Henry Meredith Edward, was born in 1872, but died in 1874. Con's sister Lady Elizabeth Edith (Betty) was born in 1867 and her other sister, Lady Emily, was born in 1874. Two sons who survived their infancy were Victor (1876-1947), and Neville (1879-1951). The children were all educated by governesses who travelled with the family to their overseas postings.

In 1880, Con returned to England when she was 11. In her memoirs, *Prisons and Prisoners,* she never refers to her early years spent abroad. In fact, she skims over almost thirty years of life in just a few brisk paragraphs. The Lyttons had decided to return to England when Robert resigned his Viceroyalty at the same time Benjamin Disraeli resigned the Premiership. Robert was then created Earl of Lytton, in the county of Derby, and Viscount of Knebworth, in the county of Hertfordshire. Betty was often her father's travelling companion and seen as the favourite child; she took on many of her mother's hostess duties as she was 'charming, gracious and confident', in what was said to be the complete opposite of Con.

Con and her sisters had a school room life with a series of governesses. She was shy and uninterested in her lessons but must have grasped a good deal in her education to write such detailed, educated letters and have later interests in prison reform and birth control. As a child she loved her animals and flowers. In India she had a parrot and then a Pekingese dog, which died around the time when her sister Betty married Gerald Balfour. She loved cleaning; a hobby she continued to perform as long as she could before her ill health prevented her.

When she was 13, she became good friends with Fraülein Oser, an Austrian lady who was a pupil of Madame Schumann. It was through Fraülein Oser that she developed a love of playing the piano and had even considered taking it up professionally and making it a career. However, by now she had replaced Betty's role as hostess to her father's dinner parties and to study music she would need to go to Austria.

In December 1887, Con moved with her family to Paris where her father was Ambassador. By now, Betty was married to Gerald Balfour, a Scottish aristocrat and Conservative MP. Gerald was the brother to the future Prime Minister, Arthur Balfour, and was also the nephew of the current Prime Minister, Lord Salisbury. Betty's sister-in-law, Frances Balfour, also became a suffrage activist. Con now regularly communicated by letter to her mother's oldest sister, Mrs Charles Earle, otherwise known as Aunt T. They regularly talked about a wide variety of subjects, despite the age difference of forty years, including flower arranging, cooking and housekeeping. Con wrote, 'What makes our talks and letters so amusing to me is that we are so totally, fundamentally different, yet sympathise over much.' Another good friend of Con's was Adela Villiers (later Mrs Francis Smith), the second daughter of her uncle Ernest Villiers and three years younger than Con. Adela was a very delicate young lady but was able to offer Con a close friendship with 'unfailing and unchanging sympathy, understanding and discretion.'

In 1890, Con's younger sister Emily wrote in a letter that Con was 'such an angel and seems to make everyone happy' apart from 'when there is someone very good near me, it seems to make me feel extra bad.'

Between 1887 and 1891, Con was in service to her family and had to take part in the social activities expected of her position as the daughter of an Ambassador, especially now that her sister, Betty, was otherwise engaged. She had to put aside her own feelings on society (she hated social functions with a passion). However, as demonstrated in her letters, she could find the funny side in many situations. On 3 June 1889 she wrote to her younger sister Emily, 'On Friday last we went to the Buckingham Palace concert...But thanks to an old gentleman who sat bang in front of us, I passed one of the most amusing evenings of my life...' The gentleman was blind and had begun whistling a tune to himself. After being told off by his wife, he whistled again, then felt for his wife and accidentally grabbed hold of Con's mother, Edith. Twice, while she was in Paris, she managed to escape the social circle and stay with Fraülein Oser, which gave Con much happiness.

A sense of duty, service and obedience was instilled in the young Con by her family. However, she shied away from the desire to embrace any public role as the daughter of a Viceroy. Instead, she preferred to embrace her love of animals and her compassionate nature developed into an empathetic desire to help those in need. Despite having physical frailties from a young age, such as frequent attacks of rheumatism, on one occasion she assisted two women she referred to as being of the 'cottage class' (someone who worked for others for wages) by helping to carry their bags for 7 miles and frequently took on some of the servants' tasks at Knebworth House.

Con's father Robert died in Paris on 24 November 1891. She wrote of her father's death, 'If my father can look into his heart, he will see there that I am happy for his sake.' He was given a state funeral in France, where Con's mother, Edith, was the chief mourner along with her surviving five children. The funeral was attended by Ministers of State, and the French government arranged for 3,500 soldiers to serve at his funeral before his body was taken by rail to England. Oscar Wilde later dedicated his play *Lady Windermere's Fan* to his memory.

A letter written by Con to Albert Broadbent, who was publishing her father's *A Lytton Treasury of Poetry*, formed the introduction to the work:

May 1909, DEAR MR BROADBENT,- You ask me to write something in memory of my father to preface the selection from his works which you are adding to your unique and most fascinating series. How can one build up in a few short sentences the magic of a personality in which gloom and radiance, the perfect and imperfect, had their part, and yet the whole was entirely revered? But his work as a poet and a statesman, and much of his private correspondence have been published, and from these the true man may be learnt, for if there is one characteristic of my father's disposition which stands out preeminently in my memory, it is his aversion to hypocrisy. In his writings, in his public career, in his private life, the bias asserts itself. It is the only thing I can recall which sometimes interfered with the generosity, even the fairness, of his judgement.

I was still young when he died, and being of a somewhat puritanical turn of mind, I was out of sympathy with several of his theories of life. I have since learnt how greatly these were due to the influences and surroundings of his youth, and I look at those theories themselves, perhaps, with a wider range of view. But even at that time of my strongest prejudice, I recognised the immense force for good of his character, and the golden-hearted generosity of his disposition. I take the following sentences from some notes made after his death, in which I tried to lay hold of those seemingly less important characteristics which are apt to fade quickly from the memory, although they so greatly charm us in a living friend.

He thought nothing of himself and always seemed surprised if admiration were shown him. Among his numerous and varied friends there were many people apparently unworthy of his friendship, in so far that in nobility and force of character, and intellectually, they were much beneath his level. When reproached, for this he would reply, 'I like those that like me,' as if the concession were towards him, and as if he were grateful for it. He never did an act of charity in the usual sense of the word. Any measured or limited kindness was impossible to his nature. If he knew of any sorrow or affliction which it was in his power to relieve, though at the time he might be overburdened with work, with difficulties and sorrows of his own, he would give himself and all that he had to his distressed friend or acquaintance – his money, his time, his strength, his sympathy. One of the things most noticeable about him was his entire want of all conventionality. Conventions were to him incomprehensible things. He could not understand them nor learn them, nor, consequently, respect them, and up to the last moment of his life they were to him as meaningless to a child of some savage race. This had its drawbacks; in the estimation of some it will be regarded as a fault never to be forgiven him. It has been said that he was more a foreigner than an Englishman. This was mainly owing to his dress, which was certainly not English; it was original, as nearly all about him, and peculiar to himself. He had lived abroad nearly all of his life. He had great sympathy with and a great admiration for the French. But he was an Englishman to his heart's core, nor could anything surpass the love he had for his own home, for his country, and for the Queen, for whose honour and service he spent his life.

CONSTANCE LYTTON

Con now felt that she had to 'adopt' her mother and take care of her, even more so as the years passed by and she remained unmarried. Knebworth was let and they moved to London, which Con was not at all keen about, finding it dark and miserable. Thankfully, Lady Bloomfield, Con's great-aunt, lent them her country house in the village of Bramfield, Hertfordshire, for the summer months. In one letter to Adela, Con describes how they came to Knebworth for the day and she found a letter addressed to her on the table from Adela, 'but the dogs said I must take them for a walk. I set forth in rain, mud and wind – three discomfits to which I am usually very sensitive – but in reading your letter I was sublimely unconscious of them all...'

During this time, Con and her mother also paid many visits to Hatfield House, including a visit during the general election of 1892.

> The rooms here are provided with the most splendidly ample stationary supplies you can possibly imagine...the whole house here is throbbing with election excitement...The good news has come in that Hertfordshire has returned a Conservative by a majority of 1,258.

In August they visited Cromer and she wrote a few lines to her sister Betty, perhaps reflecting on her father's death or current companionship to her mother 'What a mistake it is to allow oneself to care for little things, or to care for things a *little*. If one only cares enough, there is strength either to overcome every obstacle, or at least to endure every martyrdom.'

During this period, Con was described as tall, excessively spare (somewhat bony) and slender. Her features were described as refined and sensitive, with an expression of gentle melancholy. In her teenage years she was very keen on taking up music as a profession and later wanted to be a journalist. However, her parents disapproved and as such she obediently repressed these desires. Because she had been so delicate all her life and existed as a dependent daughter, she had bred within herself a fear of giving offence, was naive of character and had a pessimistic self-deprecation despite having many intellectual attributes.

In 1891, in one of her frequent letters to her brother Victor, Con wrote that she was looking forward to attending church. She had been confirmed some years before but still remembered her first Communion service and her feelings about religion had grown stronger: 'that Holy Communion is a link between us and God and calls forth all that is most divine, most elevated and most noble in our natures.' She wrote that she felt that in God, she had a friend who was always near her, who knew all her faults and weaknesses and loved her more than anyone else did. She added that by fulfilling His last commandment – the eating of bread and wine – people were doing something that pleased Him, despite it being a small thing: 'our love for Him is the only thing which can give any value to whatever determination or sacrifice we make.' She also wrote in the same letter that she was pleased to see two of her father's articles in print in the *Nineteenth Century* (one of the leading literary magazines) and the *National Review* (a platform for the views of the British Conservative Party).

In October 1892 Con sailed with her mother to Cape Town for three months so that they could visit her mother's twin sister, Lady Loch. She wrote to Adela from the RMS *Scott* on Thursday, 7 October:

> I hate the sea, I loathe a ship and everything to do with it. I can't bear wind, I detest the type of one's fellow passengers; all of these are very natural dislikes and I have not changed them, but yet I must own that two days of this voyage have been among the happy ones of my life.

Shortly after arriving, she wrote to her brother Victor describing how it felt that they were so far apart, despite it being very little time since they last saw each other. It appears she was feeling a touch of melancholy even though her mother was happier 'in spirits' since their father had died, and the Lochs were so kind to the pair of them. However, at the end of October she was writing to Adela again:

Do you know, I am more happy since I have been here, in a light-hearted, gay kind of way, than I ever remember being in my life before. All the men here are so much more courteous and sociable than in England, so that instead of dreading their presence, as I generally do, I feel quite dull when they are not there, and can laugh and joke with them from morning to night.

On Wednesday, 27 October, she met Olive Schreiner (who would later become a feminist and women's rights activist) for the first time at her home in Matjiesfontein, a small station in the Karoo Country in the Western Cape of South Africa. They would become regular letter writers to one another.

Later in November, Con wrote again to her brother Victor, describing the scenes at the Floral Fete Ceremony; an outdoor charity bazaar that she had attended. She fell in love with a 'wee pug dog', similar to Koso (one of the family's dogs), which was pulling a tiny cart. The cart was covered in ornaments, and yellow and brown flowers. The dog's harness was also covered in flowers, but he did not require leading like the goat, pony and donkey carriages, and Con thought that he looked so proud of his role during the procession. She went on to describe the trees in South Africa and how the oaks, imported by the Dutch, had sprung up fast. She was not entranced by the area and felt that there was 'none of the charm that takes hold of one' from the European scenery that she was more used to.

During these few months in South Africa, Con was happy in the sun, with bright colours, companionship, and freedom from care and responsibility. She also fell in love, although it was not destined to be, when her courtship with John (Swift) Ponsonby began. John Ponsonby was an aide de camp to Henry Loch, her godmother's husband. His father, Sir Henry Ponsonby, was an equerry to Prince Albert and was Queen Victoria's private secretary for twenty years, as well as having a distinguished military career. John Ponsonby had a hare lip and cleft palate but was tall, dark and handsome in Con's eyes. In many of her letters and diaries, she refers to John as J.P.

In 1893, Con returned with her mother to England, where they suffered from financial loss. Due to unfortunate investments, any savings that her father, Lord Lytton, had had were now lost, and Lady Lytton and Con had to resign themselves to the fact that they now had to live a modest life, or as Lady Betty referred to it in *Letters of Constance Lytton* 'a condition of comparative poverty'. Olive Schreiner wrote to Con but sent the letter via Adela because she did not know Con's address, as Con and her mother (while not in attendance to the Queen) were flitting between friends and families' properties at this time.

Between 1893 and 1901, Edith rented a small property about 12 miles from Knebworth called 'The Danes'. It was at the edge of a large park and Con was relieved that they were no longer living in London. Here she concentrated on looking after her mother and communicating with the rest of the family. They had to reduce their household, hoping that they could still keep her brother Neville at Eton and also still live within their means. Con even resorted to visiting a pawnbroker in London to sell some 'rubbishy old bits of Indian jewelry', for which she received £7. She used this money to help purchase a revolving bookcase that her mother had much coveted, but had said that they must not think of luxuries at that time. That summer, Con wrote to Adela with the news that 'our money man has gone smash altogether, and not a penny of the money can be saved (except a very little from some Turkish bond securities, but no one thinks these worth anything).' She also met up with her friend Olive Schreiner during the summer, her mother having said to Con, 'If only you *would* [not *could*] find a man just like her to marry.' She felt inclined to answer, 'I'll take the pattern to Whiteley's tomorrow and try to match it.'

As well as books and letter writing, Con was also a fan of art. She mentioned to Neville that her sister Betty and her husband, Gerald, would despise the Grafton Exhibitions because they were blind to the French Impressionist School, although Con felt that it had merit and that the showing of the pictures would do good for the art world, despite the art school being a little bit in advance of the times.

Additionally, Con was a great animal lover and wrote fondly about the dogs of the house: 'Gobble is just lifting up his voice very aggressively because Mother has promised, most virtuously, to take him a turn before church.' Tippoo, also known as Fuzzy Wuzzy, was a large black cat who liked to steal food off the plates at mealtimes, often leaving her still hungry after tea. Gobble and Kush, Victor's dogs, liked to lick the plates clean after pudding. When Con tried to brush them, they would merely put their hairless face to the brush and would instead lie on their matted parts so she could not reach them. Sometimes she was left home alone with the animals, which she did not mind. Gobble was Neville's dog and saw Con as his deputy master, and rather than sleeping in the servants' quarters, as was the norm, he retreated to Con's room. He slept on her bed while she was away, hiding underneath it until he thought it was safe, before panicking at discovering a live person under the covers when she went to pat him.

Meanwhile, Con was very excited at the prospect of her brother Victor heading off to Cambridge, hoping that he would feel he was really beginning to live there. She had herself just finished writing an article (a book review) that she thought would be impossible to write, but managed it anyway. Her work came to her in batches, and she had lots of 'play time' in between the articles she was writing of her own accord. If she decided she had had enough of the work, then she could put her foot down and say no more, and no one would mind. She also tried to write up stories, some from the skeleton of ideas thought up by Betty, thinking she might be able to 'turn a penny or live by it' from the results.

Con described The Danes as being a cosy, homely, delightful place. She loved the creepers outside and thought the kitchen garden was splendid. The Danes had two tennis lawns, good-sized bedrooms and a room that was called the library, but only had only three books in it, of which one was by the philosopher Bernard Bosanquet. Con also sometimes stayed with Betty at 67 Addison Road in Kensington, but some of the guests who visited wanted to discuss 'the charm and merriment of gown conversation at the ball', which was not Con's cup of tea at all.

In January 1893, Con and her mother, whom she often referred to as Muddy, went to see the sculptor Sir Alfred Gilbert, who was working on a monument to her father for St Paul's Cathedral. The memorial, which is now in the crypt of the cathedral, is cast in bronze and marble and depicts two women bearing a portrait of a man, with a winged child below it. Con helped draft the below inscription:

Edward Robert Bulwer-Lytton

First Earl of Lytton Viscount Knebworth P.C. G.C.B. C.C.S.I. C.I.E.

Born November VIII MDCCCXXXI

From MDCCCL to MDCCCLXXVI in the diplomatic service of his country. From MDCCCLXXXVII to the day of his death, ambassador of Paris where he died November XXIV MDCCCXCI. He was a diplomat rich in the qualities official and social by which amity with foreign nations is maintained. A Viceroy independent in his views, resolute in action, looking forward to the future. A poet of many styles each the expression of his habitual thoughts. A man of superior faculties highly cultivated by literature, ardent in his affections, tender & generous in all the circumstances of life, lavish in his commendations of others & humble in his estimate of himself.

The family muddled on and in August 1893 Con wrote one of her regular letters to Aunt T and touched on the subject of votes for women for possibly the first time.

> On the subject of the Women's Movement, I hardly know what I agree with. I get so angry with the old-fashioned man's woman, and so furious with the advanced woman who goes in for women's *superiority* over men, and so enraged with the people who demand *equality* for men and women, not in the sense of justice and fairness, but meaning *sameness*, which I think wildly impossible and unnatural for such differently constituted beings. My all-round rage with these makes me too giddy to form sound opinions of my own.

Later in 1893, Con was socialising with Lady Ponsonby, John's mother, and his sister Maggie. She had been invited to spend a week at the Ponsonby's Scotland home, just 3 miles from Balmoral Castle, and from there she would go on to stay with her sister Betty at Whittinghame.

A biography that appeared in the *Wigton Advertiser* on 16 December 1893 gives a description of Con at this time:

> LADY CONSTANCE LYTTON. One of the contributors to the Christmas number of Woman is Lady Constance Lytton, a daughter of the late Lord Lytton, who is only 24 years of age, and has, it appears, taken to press work in earnest. This titled lady journalist had some experience in India. When Lord Lytton was Viceroy he started a little magazine for the

occupation and amusement of his children, who wrote for and conducted it themselves. This periodical was, in fact, the organ of a private society of English children in India. This society held a weekly council somewhat on the lines of its prototype, the Vice-Regal Cabinet, at which solemn discussions were held as to the policy of the organisation. If members did not attend, a time was imposed, and, as a society could not exist without funds, certain bazaars and art exhibitions were held with a view to raising money. The magazine itself, however, was produced without much expense, as the Government printer worked loyally and gratuitously for the family of the Viceroy. Among the features of the magazine were prizes offered for various kinds of puzzles.

Two years later, in early 1895, Mr Earl Hodgson, editor of *The Realm*, offered Con a post on his paper. She took the job temporarily and wrote excitedly to Aunt T:

OFFICE OF *The Realm*, NORFOLK STREET, STRAND Me! Think of it, in an office! The quiet and uninterruptedness is too blissful to be true, and I am most comfortably provided for Mr Earl Hodgson has been more kind than words can say.

Further letters describe how much she was enjoying her work, staying up until 2 am working before rising again at 7 to walk to the station and not returning home until 9. This was a short career reviewing novels for the *National Review* and the *Realm*, from which she earned a regular salary. During this period, she would lunch frugally on ginger biscuits and brown bread and despite working into the small hours, the work made her feel 'rampantly well'. She felt she could not lay claim to the money she earned, so instead bought presents for her mother and then paid for her sister Emily's travel expenses. Unfortunately, despite the journalism position offering over £100 a year, Con relinquished the situation as it was taking her away from home too much, which Edith disapproved of. However, in Con's eyes, she gave it up just as obligingly as she had given up playing the piano professionally.

Chapter 2

Relationship with John Ponsonby and Maurice Baring, 1897-1908

As we have seen, in 1892 Con went to South Africa to visit her aunt and whilst there met a man called John Ponsonby, who was working as an aide de camp for her uncle, the bush commissioner. Although born with a cleft palate and a hare lip, these were barely distinguishable as John covered them with a bushy moustache. However, Constance found him adorable and during their time together in South Africa they spoke of marriage, but the problem was that both had no money to speak of.

Once back in England, Edith strongly discouraged communication between the two of them but occasionally lifted the ban, temporarily raising Con's hopes. The Ponsonby family also entertained Con, further encouraging her to believe that a match may be possible, although John was still stationed in South Africa. Con would avidly watch the news from each country John was posted to, which included Uganda and Niger. She would also write regularly about him in her diary and mention him frequently in her letters to friends and family.

In a letter to her best friend and cousin Adela Villiers in 1900, Con describes herself as not just a submissive woman but as a victim, saying:

> I think I'm by nature constructed more like an Eastern woman than a European, with a thick proportion of slavish instincts in my blood. What I hunger for most is to be able to serve those I love. I don't want their respect, but that they should *need* me,

whether as a servant, or a toy, or a wife [perhaps referring here to her on/off relationship with John].

Con frequently slipped into a depression, feeling almost lifeless, which could only be revived by word of or by him. These low moments generally triggered a desire to be alone, particularly later while at Homewood with her mother: 'The only wish I can define offhand as being chronically there is to be alone, in fact, simply to be able to go my own way regardless of anyone else.' Freedom and an independent life, alone, was something she deeply desired, but sadly nearly every wish of hers was accompanied by 'the certainty that it will be disapproved against [which] acts like a cold wind'. She added that 'My wishes [Edith] studied only to oppose them, it being a kind of accepted thing that if I want a thing it's bad for me and therefore to be refused...it's the kind of attitude behind everything which gets on one's nerves at times.' Then adding, 'she does it entirely for my good yet nothing could have been much further from what I like'. Con resorted to writing to her Aunt T of being treated like a 'semi-maniac' by her mother. Although Con did not want to hurt Edith, insisting that 'it would be impossible to do anything which would give her acute moral pain', she still later went ahead with her militant activities; the prison sentences in particular causing Edith much anguish.

Con conversed frequently with her Aunt T and the question of freedom was often a point of discussion between the two correspondents. Her aunt had asked Con what she would do if she were 'quite free'. Con replied that she would be a vegetarian. She did later take up vegetarianism (her aunt was also vegetarian) and it provided her with the means to exert control over one aspect of her life. However, this lifestyle would later prove to be a challenge both at home and in prison.

Aunt T disapproved of the role of the 'caged daughter', a position that Con felt she was in, describing it as:

A thing of which I should have had the greatest horror if I had had daughters of my own. I think no parents have any right to trammel the lives of grown-up daughters. Why should women be more or less slaves because they do not happen to marry?

Con took the point up with her brother Victor, too:

Mothers who allow their daughters freedom have remarked 'how absurd it is to talk as if mothers tyrannised over their daughters like that' and the mothers who look upon their daughters only as untrustworthy slaves have said 'how can anyone make such a ridiculous proposal as that daughters should have any interests, occupations or friends except those which their parents select for them.' It seems to me that the only cases in which it would be justifiable for a daughter to 'revolt' (as it is called), i.e. make a stand in her own interests against her parents' wishes, are the cases when such a revolt would be utterly useless – impossible in fact...they have to conform themselves very often to the narrow life of practically an unpaid servant.

John Ponsonby occasionally returned to England for short periods, and on one of these occasions, Con worried that she did not possess an outfit 'that isn't acutely hideousifying'. She also wanted to conceal from John the extent of her passion. She wrote to a friend once that she had 'hardly talked to him' but also wrote that she had started to fantasise about sleeping with him out of wedlock, although she could not bear to think of how Edith would take it, should she bear a child, again wanting to avoid giving her mother 'moral pain'. Edith continued to press on Con that she must give John up. To everyone's relief, except Con's, John let it be known to the Lytton family that he had fallen in love with someone else.

In May 1894, Con wrote to her sister Betty about the problems she was experiencing with their mother. She believed that her mother had thought Con had resigned herself to being an old maid and would never marry, but once she discovered that Con did indeed want to marry, she reawakened all her highest hopes and ambitions for such an event. However, Con did not want to marry into an intellectual atmosphere and have duties thrust upon her that were dependent upon wealth or rank. Con knew that John Ponsonby had his faults, and that her mother thought he was not of a high enough rank to be suitable for her daughter, but she loved him anyway.

In late 1894 Betty had conversed with her friend Evelyn regarding Con's situation with John Ponsonby and had recounted the conversation to Con in a letter. The initial discussion between Betty and Evelyn was whether children should be left enough money to live in the position to which they were born. Sons were expected to earn their own living, but spinster daughters, such as Con and Emily, would have just £200 a year should their mother die. Con could, of course, be a companion, but Evelyn suggested that Con be allowed to marry someone considered 'poor', even though in the future, John would receive a sizeable inheritance as the eldest son. Betty felt that this was a comforting suggestion, but it is a pity that Edith did not agree.

Betty wrote to Con again following a conversation they had had over John Ponsonby earlier that morning. She had discussed the situation with her husband Gerald, and he had thought of a suggestion that he would put to Edith when he next saw her. John had said that he would consult his own parents as to the matter in hand. Gerald advised that Con should write to him and urge him to do so at once and then inform her as soon as possible as to what they had said. Gerald also said that if the response was what was expected – that marriage was out of the question – then they should both consider each other free. Gerald stated that he feared John might give a doubtful answer as to his parents' views, and in this case, Edith should demand a clearer response from his parents.

Betty wrote again to Con saying that she had told Maggie (John's sister) that if he tried to find out the state of Con's feelings from her (Maggie), she would conceal the facts. Betty had bumped into John as she came away from St James', and he had said that he would come and visit, yet he had not done so. Betty said that she was having a party and asked whether she should invite Con and John. Betty also mentioned Lady Ponsonby, John's mother, in her letters, saying that she spoke a lot about Con and John, although separately writing, 'she's delicious about you and raved of you'.

In further letters to Con, Betty stated that Aunt T was writing depressing letters regarding Con, saying that her (Con's) happiness was forced, and that 'Mother's conduct is inexplicable and the Ponsonbys' conduct most blamable'. Con's illness at this time had crept back again and she described in one of her shorter letters to friends how she was desperate for things to make her happy, such as puppies and flowers. The discomfort of her body, from a weak heart and rheumatic bouts, was still very dreadful, and she did not want anyone to see her like that.

In May 1895 Edith took Con and her sister Emily to Florence, where they experienced a severe earthquake. Con wrote to Aunt T 'This letter is written hot from a scene the most uncanny and awe-inspiring that I have ever witnessed,' before going on to describe what had happened to the family during the earthquake. It was in Florence that she first met Maurice Baring, whose father was part of the Baring banking family. Maurice was also a nephew of Lady Ponsonby, and before long he was to become a well-known writer, diplomat and man of letters, writing journalism, poetry, plays and novels. Con may have had a romantic interest in Maurice, writing to her sister Betty that if 'ever my matters run smooth and banns are published, wedding arranged etc…that I shall be waiting at the church…and that the other person will never turn up.'

In June 1895 Edith Lytton received a letter inviting her to become a lady in waiting to Queen Victoria:

MY DEAR LADY LYTTON-

A vacancy has occurred amongst my ladies-in-waiting caused by an event which has grieved me deeply, viz, the death of my dear and valued friend the Dowager Duchess of Roxburghe, and I would like to offer it to you. Having known so many of your family for so long, several of them having been, and still being in my household, and having a grateful sense of your husband's distinguished services, as well as a sincere admiration of the way in which you have borne your sorrows and trials, it would give me much pleasure if you would accept this offer. Hoping soon to hear from you. Believe me always yours affectionately. VICTORIA R.I.

For taking on this post Edith received £300 per year and served with eight other aristocratic maids of honour. Her new duties took her away from home about four times a year for about a fortnight at a time. These periods away gave Con some of the solitude that she was always craving. Writing from The Danes to Aunt T, Con stated 'One of the joys of being alone is that I can get rid of unshed tears that have accumulated for months…nothing does one so much good now and then. It's like having at last an opportunity to wash one's only shirt…'

Con worried a great deal about her best friend Adela because of her frailty, and wrote many letters describing these worries, including one written from Waterloo station in the summer of 1896. In it, she described how, having just seen Adela, 'she's still far from well I fear & suffers horribly from neuralgia, rheumations & swollen gland.

Dr calls it remains of mumps.' Adela was to come to Woodlands, where Con was also staying, the following day for a change and some country air.

Con was also able to unload her own worries to her friend, as seen in a letter to Adela from July 1896, when she wrote:

> I've been having a most sickening time with myself. Can't think what it is that suddenly lets me down to the lowest depths without a word of warning...My beastly body is so tired, I can't get it to work at all...I'm dead tired and I'm going to bed with all my duties undone...Your dead sick CON.

A couple of months later she wrote to Adela again assuring her that 'I'm nowhere *near* dying if that's what you're haunted by – and I swear I'll send you a postcard if ever the spirit moves me that way.'

In October 1896 Con travelled to the Chief Secretary's Lodge at Phoenix Park, in Dublin. Gerald, her brother-in-law, was Chief Secretary for Ireland between 1895 and 1900, when Lord Cadogan was Viceroy. In a letter to Aunt T she said, 'I am quite in love with this Irish place...I do love the kindness and genial civility too, in streets, shops etc...' She enjoyed watching a parade of the Irish Constabulary and had lunch with Lord Dufferin's daughter, Lady Plunket. Betty would later write in her *Letters of Constance Lytton* that 'After a spell of unusual depression and physical lethargy, the joy of life would return to Con for no external cause. Gropingly she felt that happiness, not sadness, was meant to go with the gift of life.' However, Con's letters during these years often described her desire to return home from wherever she happened to be staying, as she longed for some solicitude.

Two months later, in December 1896, Con's relationship with John Ponsonby was potentially referenced again when Olive Schreiner wrote in a letter to her that:

It is the tragedy which arises when a man cannot really love a woman <u>because she is too much his superior</u>; intellectually and emotionally she moves in a higher world than that in which he <u>can</u> move. It would kill him to live always in her atmosphere. A sparrow <u>cannot</u> live up in the air where an eagle breathes easily! (*Olive Schreiner Letters Project*)

Con was a prolific letter writer and in 1896 collaborated with her Aunt T on her book *Potpourri from a Surrey Garden*, published in 1897. Chapters from the book were sent to Con periodically for her to read and criticise before publication. The idea for the book came when Con was staying at Aunt T's house recovering from an attack of measles, and a foreign friend of her aunt's came to stay and asked for advice about gardening. Aunt T dictated notes on the subject to Con, which soon formed the basis of a book. Aunt T wrote 'But for my niece and her help, it would never have been finished, and, but for her it would probably have been consigned to the flames, as I feared my husband did not like my publishing it.'

Con wrote to her brother Victor in February 1897 about how exciting it was that Aunt T's book was nearly finished and that she, Con, could not do or think of anything else. However, she recommended that he look at Olive Schreiner's latest book, *Trooper Peter Halket of Mashonaland*, as Con wanted to discuss the contents. The book in question was a novella about the complex political situation in South Africa and the greedy rush for mineral exploitation at the expense of the native Africans.

Con spent the money she received from helping with her aunt's book on herself; the first time she had rewarded herself for something. However, Aunt T somehow made her feel guilty for doing so, so she vowed to pay her back, even though Con had calculated that in the time she had been working on the manuscript for the book, she could have lawfully earned the same amount of money by other means.

Relationship with John Ponsonby and Maurice Baring, 1897-1908

In 1897 Con's younger sister, Emily, was married to the renowned architect Edwin Lutyens, and in the same year her brother Victor came of age. Although the family were living at The Danes and Knebworth House was let out, there was still a party under a tent in the park of the Knebworth Estate grounds. Con travelled down to London in advance of the party to buy Victor a smart tie for the occasion, and she must have been particularly excited as *Potpourri from a Surrey Garden* was about to be reprinted in its third edition, but equally saddened as her own love life was not exactly progressing.

Con enjoyed talking to different people wherever she went, regardless of their situation in life, as can be seen in a letter she wrote to Adela:

> I tried to begin this while waiting for the train, but then a nursing mother and babe turned up and were so interesting so I had to stop. The mother confided to me, before five minutes had gone by, that the baby was 'an accident', and how she had no father and mother, but that the father of the child had behaved very well about it, and she was so deliciously pleased with her baby and seemed so refreshingly light-hearted about the 'accident' part of it. Yet she looked ultra good and respectable and *very* ugly. She probably hardly knows how to scrape along from day to day, but one couldn't help feeling almost envious in spite of all the drawbacks. She earns about three shillings a week by making pillow lace and is strong and well.

In 1899, Con helped her Aunt T with a second potpourri book, despite the conflicts that had arisen over the first one, and wrote to her saying:

> What I think is almost unique about your books is your attitude to yourself, the honesty of it. If your readers will take a hint

from that, it will be more helpful to them than all the useful information in the book, good as that is. I feel that is what has been more valuable to me than anything else in my intercourse with you. I have tried to practise what I learn from it, and shall go on trying.

Coupled with the success of these two books and her journalistic attempts, it is possible that this will have given Con the confidence to write her important book and articles on prison reform/votes for women later in life.

Carrying on with her themes of important topics in her many letters, Con also discussed the trials faced by women in a letter to her sister Betty:

For aught you or I know, I may become an electioneering propagandist woman...or anything else, before the next run out. But this is unlikely, and I've reached that place in the lane of life when the probable alternatives of the future are fairly visible. I can't honestly say they please me much, but how few people are really pleased, and there are worse trials than mine in nearly every life I know. I get to like human beings better every year, and this makes life extremely interesting. But it seems like *waiting*, not actually *living*...The company of Nell and Mary [her sister's children] all to myself makes even the waiting attitude extremely bearable at this moment.

Little did Con know what awaited her in the future.

When Queen Victoria died in 1901, Con described witnessing the funeral in a letter to Aunt T, stating 'I thought Saturday was the most choking and impressive public thing I've ever seen.' Betty later described in her book how Queen Alexandra had given Edith the In Memoriam Brooch at Windsor and hoped that she would continue on as 'her lady'. Edith had replied saying that although she would do anything for Her Majesty, she feared she was too old and 'worn out'. However, she nevertheless continued as a lady in waiting for the new queen until 1905.

On 5 May 1901 Con wrote a sad letter to Betty describing how life at Homewood with her mother was quiet and how she was frequently confined to bed with bouts of rheumatic fever, while her siblings were busy with their own independent lives:

> I gather from yours to Mother and to me that you ache for me in what you suppose must be my craving for interests, to feel myself of use, the need of something to love, or at any rate for something to love me, and make one feel tied to life.
>
> If you knew how far this is from the truth! I've no yearning of any sort whatever. In a way it's most divinely peaceful after a sort of chronic hunger for years...It's as if all desires, all interest, had been removed, like an animal's body trussed and boned. I suppose it's not likely that this will last, and yet it's so like what I remember I used to feel, I half suspect it may be my own true nature reasserting myself...

In October 1901, Con was hoping that Pamela Plowden, a friend of her brother Victor's, could come to stay with her at Woodlands. She asked Aunt T if this would be possible, and her aunt replied that she would be 'delighted,' but that she would require Edith's 'sanction'. So, Con asked her mother, who surprisingly responded by saying that she did mind, and that she did not wish for Con to make friends with Pamela. There were rumours of a possible historic liaison between Pamela's mother and Con's father, which is perhaps why Edith was not keen on Victor and Pamela marrying, but she said she would make the best of it if they did. In the meantime, a friendship between Con and Pamela, or even Pamela and Edith, would only help the situation. Edith added that 'It's just what the Ponsonbys did to you – I always thought it unkind & foolish – I won't do the same by any girl.' Edith was probably also sympathetic to the fact that John Ponsonby's sisters had developed a friendship with Con, blindly leading her on, despite there apparently being no chance that the two would marry. Nevertheless, despite Edith's actions, Pamela and Victor married the following year at St Margaret's in Westminster.

In 1902 Con fell seriously ill with an acute rheumatic attack. Although she had adopted a vegetarian diet, which had been recommended to her by Aunt T and had appeared to help her rheumatism, she was still laid up in bed for some time. Con's health had never been good throughout her life; prior to joining the Suffragettes, she ate very little, was picky about her food and worried a lot.

In her memoir *Prisons and Prisoners*, Con refers to her continuing fragile health and her gentle temperament: 'I was an average human being,' she wrote 'except perhaps with an exaggerated dislike of society and publicity in any form.' Indeed, historians have often been puzzled as to how someone with such an aversion to society and publicity could have campaigned for women's suffrage and prison reform as Con did between 1909 and 1912.

From the summer of 1902, Con and Edith lived together at Homewood, a draughty dower house (a moderate home for use by the widow of the previous owner) on the Knebworth estate. Homewood, built in 1902, was far more modest than Knebworth. It had been designed in the Arts and Crafts style by Edwin Lutyens, Con's brother-in-law. Lutyens' biographer mentions that he had seen Homewood as a doll's house, but his children always spent their Easter holidays there. It had been mentioned that there were oil lamps dotted about the house and that Edith insisted on taking hip baths. There was one bathroom, but this was used by Con, particularly during her later invalid years. In the process of moving house, Con glanced through her many letters and jotted a line about this to her Aunt T:

> It's as if I were dead and were going over my past from the point of view of another life. For the most part all these letters fill me with thankfulness about now. How much more instructive and interesting they are than any book! This turn has determined me more than ever to keep letters.

Thankfully, many of Con's letters were kept and they provide a fascinating insight into her life and thoughts, particularly her interest into prison reform and votes for women.

Con was a correspondent of Edward Marsh and wrote to congratulate him when he took on the role of Private Secretary to Winston Churchill, who at the time was Under-Secretary of State for the Colonies. She wished him luck in his new line of work and said of his boss: 'The first time you see Winston Churchill you see all his faults, and the rest of your life you spend discovering his virtues.' She had clearly developed an early interest in politics, possibly peaked by her brother's entrance into the profession, and later even owned a picture by Churchill.

Maurice Baring was another of Con's male friends, and the two had first met in Florence in 1895. In 1903, Maurice wrote to Con asking if she was done reviewing the proofs of his recent piece and, if so, would she return them to him. He said he had enjoyed his evening at Woodlands very much, particularly their walks and talks together. He was off to stay at Rake in Milford, Surrey where her younger brother Neville and his wife Judith Blunt lived. It is hard to ascertain how deep their relationship was, but Con took as much interest in his work and travels as she had done with John Ponsonby.

In a letter to Pamela from February 1903, Con said that she would be going to stay with Adela at 4 Gloucester Place in Portman Square and then onwards to stay indefinitely with Betty, her sister. She stated that she was getting on splendidly but was still bad with walking and felt 'utterly brainless'.

During August 1903 Con wrote to Pamela describing how she had been playing lawn tennis with the children and then went motoring in the afternoon, but the car had broken down at Chelmsford. In her next letter, Con mentioned Maurice Baring bringing some 'heavenly fascinating' photographs on the Saturday. Con described how she had difficulty in choosing the best photographs of the children, as the best one of 'Babe' (presumably Antony, Victor and Pamela's son, who was born in 1903) was not a good photograph of Pamela. Con had numbered the images on the back and said that Aunt T would like some too. She went on to say how she had spent a heavenly Sabbath with Maurice there, who had told heavenly anecdotes about John Ponsonby and his family, and she felt warmed as a result. She added that Maurice was bringing out a new book of plays soon and that he seemed busy.

Pamela must have written back to Con regarding John Ponsonby, as Con had written again to her detailing that she had 'had such a heavenly food-full time of news about him lately'. But talking about Maurice Baring also gave her a gnarled lump in the throat and she felt that repressing these feelings made her look ill in the face. Aunt T would question Con about her feelings, but her resilience on this front left her life feeling dreary. Con was obviously full of conflicting thoughts between the two men, but in late October 1903, she wrote further to Pam saying that the family wanted her to avoid speculation regarding her and John, but her heart was still lamenting after him. Con was kept busy at this time of much anguish by helping her mother look after her nephew. She loved children and they loved her.

Later, in November 1903, Con was staying with Betty in Whittinghame, Prestonkirk, East Lothian. While she was away her mother had organised a shoot back home and had entertained guests.

Con reflected that she was sad her mother did not have guests to entertain that often. Edith was, after all, a lady in waiting to the Queen. Con also described how she had climbed a nearby hill with her sister, and while doing so, had had a long discussion with her about Scottish novels and that the two combined efforts had left her feeling wiped out. Con also reported to her mother that she felt her sister's family, the Balfour tribe, were senseless to their effects on ordinary people, and did not conceal things they did that they might have been ashamed of. Consequently, Con felt that she could talk about the Balfour family freely without her own shame.

Con's interest in political matters continued into the New Year. In February 1904 she wrote that she was upset at the suggestion Chamberlain was merely an imperialist of the baser commercial kind and that he was being condemned. In mid-March, Con received a letter from Maurice, who at the time was in Russia, apparently having a contented and thrilling time there. In April, she heard that he was going to Manchuria as a war correspondent for the *Morning Post*. 'Disheartening to his friends although good for him,' she said. 'He is a real joy corner in my life wherein I can dig and play and do no harm to anyone. I have a feeling of perhaps rather exaggerated gratitude to him for this.' She loved reading Maurice's articles in the *Morning Post* and reported about them eagerly to her Aunt T: 'I think he builds new hinterlands behind a point in the lives of well-known folk, in a most masterly and imaginative way.' Con and Maurice wrote to each other frequently, but many of the letters have since been destroyed, leading one to wonder at what they might have contained. It would be nice to think that the two of them had some sort of relationship, as the family left them alone together frequently and it is obvious that Maurice cared about her a great deal, even helping her sister Betty with her book of letters after Con's death.

During mid-October 1904, a funny incident happened in Con's presence worthy of discussion in a letter. The politician Baillie

Hamilton had come for tea, and her nephew Antony, had insisted that Baillie was Dada:

> He did have breeches on and a generally more manly appearance than anything that's been in the drawing room for ages but twas trying all the same. He said, 'hip hip' to the man and was miserable when he left & rejected him the following night.

She wrote further and said that Antony's intelligence was certainly abnormally well-developed, and that he might be a Lord Acton in the future.

During mid-March 1905, Con found her time alone surpassing all expectations; it made her good tempered, everything became very pleasant, and she found her solitude a good companion. Her only trouble at the time appeared to be her dog, who after his bath, went and worshipped a dead rat so she had to clean him again.

In May of that year, Con sent Victor some books, including the *Mosely Commission*, and her favourite Emerson book, in which she felt that the essay on intellect would produce some good ideas. She had also marked the heroism essay with notes, asking if he could return these treasured books when he was finished with them. A week later, a carriage came from Bramfield with a note saying that Aunt Georgy was very ill and would Edith come at once. The Balfour children were at Homewood for a week, but poor Edith would probably not see much of them. All was soon over, however, and Aunt Georgy passed away after much pain across her chest and her breathing had become laboured and heavy. Con was able to kiss her goodbye shortly after. It seems that heart problems were to run in Con's family.

During July 1905, Con wrote to Pamela from Woodlands, reporting that Adela was poorly again and that both Con and Aunt T had been discussing treatment plans. Maurice had come to stay for a night before he went back to Russia. Con declared that she would feel flat when he went away again, and that he was connected to everything that was rousing and hallowed in her life. A further letter from Con to Pamela states that she had not heard from Maggie Ponsonby, John's sister, nor did she expect to. Once Con's relationship with John had ended, Maggie had lost all interest in Con, who stated that she had become accustomed to it. Later, in early December 1905, Con wrote that she had had 'a most heavenly letter from Maurice Baring', and that she hoped someone would see to it that he did not go back to Russia without a fur coat. A few months later, in early 1906, Pamela offered to lend Con her motor car so that Con and Maurice could take a picnic lunch and spend the day by a lake. Edith did not appear to mind lunching alone – was this an approval? In the same year, Con's godmother and great-aunt, Lady Bloomfield, died and left her some money. It was this bequest that later led Con to meeting the Suffragettes.

During August 1905, Con was upset to hear about Victor's recent ailments. Her other brother, Neville, had also been ill some time before but he had treated himself with Haig's dietetics. Con related her findings regarding the taking of aspirin and soda to Victor. She suggested that a beneficial effect should be found after the first or second dose, but if the tablets did not work or if they disagreed with him, then they should be 'left off and purged since they could cause indigestion and pain'. Con declared that she could not take these tablets during the day as they affected her circulation and made ordinary life an effort, but she could take small quantities in the evening. If she felt biliousness, she was forced to go without food and to bed. Con said that Edith believed Turkish baths could help against depression caused by London life, but her own hopes were solely to make her hygiene easier, and her disablement and pain less severe. She believed that she might finally be gaining ground after becoming a vegetarian and that diet had played a large part in helping her to achieve this.

The following year, on 9 May 1907, Con wrote that she had had a little walk with Maurice at Woodlands, and that Aunt T had humbly withdrawn herself for most of that afternoon. Con sent her friend Olive Schreiner a book, *A Year in Russia*, written by her 'journalist friend of much talent'. The book itself was dedicated to Lady Constance Lytton.

For reasons unknown, in June 1907 Con wrote the outlines of a will and gave it to Betty. She intended to leave her Aunt T the money that came to Con from her, but if Aunt T passed away beforehand, then this money would go to Lionel (a cousin) and others. She would leave her fortune from Lady Bloomfield to John Ponsonby, as well as any other additional money that Con had come into. Con also wrote that she was leaving her jewels, books and other pieces, including those mentioned in her father's will, to Betty to dispose of as per the instructions in a letter written to her, and that she chose Betty, Victor and Neville to be her successors. For some strange reason, there is no mention of her sister Emily in the will.

In the following February, Olive Schreiner sent a copy of Edward Carpenter's pamphlet, possibly *British Aristocracy and the House of Lords,* to Con for her to read after she had been bed-bound for a few weeks thanks to influenza. Con had previously read Carpenter's book *Love's Coming of Age,* a short collection of essays about gender roles, equality and the stifling nature of marriage at the start of the twentieth century and had said that it was her best companion. Reading this book and pamphlet was beginning to open Con's mind towards equality between men and women. Schreiner, by this point, had also become the Vice President of the Cape branch of the Women's Enfranchisement League and was possibly trying to influence Con through her choice of reading material.

Chapter 3

Becoming a Suffragette, 1908

By the early twentieth century, British campaigners had been arguing for votes for women for decades, and it was only when a large number of suffragists faced despair after their peaceful methods of protest had failed that they decided their methods needed to turn to militancy by breaking laws in pursuit of their aims. Many of these newly christened 'Suffragettes' were taken to Holloway prison, where they were treated as common criminals as opposed to political prisoners, which is how they saw themselves.

According to Betty Balfour's *Letters of Constance Lytton*, Con had no interest in women's suffrage until it entered her personal life. The Women's Social and Political Union (WSPU), which Con eventually joined, was also known as the Militant Suffrage Society and was founded in 1903 by Emmeline and Christabel Pankhurst in Manchester. In 1906, Mrs Henry Fawcett, leader of the National Union of Women's Suffrage Societies, had made a deputation, along with all the women's suffrage societies, to Prime Minister Sir Henry Campbell-Bannerman, and in her memoirs, she said:

> After this for several years the whole country, indeed we might almost say the whole world, rang with the doings of the Suffragettes, as the violent Suffragists came to be called. I would point out, however, that for at least two years of their activity, 1906-8, while they suffered extraordinary acts of physical violence, they used none, and all through, from beginning to

end of their campaign, they took no life, and shed no blood, either of man or beast.

Con did not become involved with the Suffragettes until a chance meeting in the summer of 1908. The term 'Suffragette' was first used by the *Daily Mail* newspaper in 1906 as a way of mocking those involved. However, the women it targeted decided to adopt the name for the title of one of the newspapers published by the WSPU.

Prior to joining the group, in January 1907 Con had written at length to her Aunt T about the suffrage deputation:

> I am so surprised at your having refused to sign a paper backing woman's suffrage. I thought you were for it! Perhaps you have many reasons against it, but those you give in your letter for not signing I think are very poor in themselves. 1. That it is being taken up by the Conservative Party, 2. That you think some things are of greater importance.
>
> I don't see how by any stretch the question can be made a party one. If everyone refused to record an opinion except on the subject they thought first in importance, things would get rather stuck. There is nothing, is there, in Woman Suffrage that would be anti-disarmament or anti any of the other causes you have at heart?
>
> I am for it. I am impressed by practically all the arguments for it, and I have never yet heard an argument against it which I thought convincing. I think its advantages and alterations would be chiefly indirect! The increased responsibility would be good for the females I think, and their increased power would be good for the men. The countries in which the women are the least legally recognised tend to disregard their interests and to be in all ways rather retrograde, I think.

Con's first encounter with the suffrage movement began when she had decided she wished to dedicate the money from Lady Bloomfield, which she had inherited in 1906, to a public cause. Her brother Neville introduced her to a movement for the revival of Morris dancing and folk singing and it was through this that she was introduced to Mary Neal, the secretary of a North London working girls' club, the Espérance Club. The club and the Maison Espérance dressmaking co-operative had been founded in the mid-1890s by Emmeline Pethick-Lawrence and Mary Neal as a response to discovering distressing conditions for girls employed in the London dress trade. The club was based at 50 Cumberland Market in the St Pancras district of London and was open every night of the week. Mary Neal had an interest in folk songs and dance songs collected by Cecil Sharp, and she invited some traditional dancers to teach Morris dancing to the young women who attended the club. This in turn inspired the New Espérance Morris group, which demonstrated their dances across the country and later danced at some of the WSPU events.

In 1908, Con, now aged 39, took a holiday by the sea at Littlehampton in Sussex. She had accepted her friend Mary Neal's offer to spend the summer at the Espérance Club's Green Lady Hostel, which had been set up by Mary in 1900. The hostel was just off East Street in Littlehampton and was run by a folk and Morris dancer revivalist between the 1900s and 1940s as accommodation for working women from London, such as factory workers. A pioneer of working women's holidays, the hostel welcomed women of all ages, means and churches. Mary Neal believed that folk dancing, such as Morris dancing, would help women to express themselves and ultimately give them the confidence to improve their lives. Her belief was to free working-class women from servitude, and the girls were all invited to teach in villages, schools and factories across England. Con decided to donate her £1,000 legacy from Lady Bloomfield to the club after the dancers had performed in Knebworth.

Three of Con's housemates that summer were Suffragettes: Emmeline Pethick-Lawrence, and Annie and Jessie Kenney, the latter of whom had only just been released from Holloway, having been imprisoned for a month after taking part in a demonstration at Parliament Square. Jessie and Con talked about the humiliating conditions for women who were inmates in Holloway. Writing shortly after to her friend Adela, Con described how she 'got knotted up with suffragettes' and appeared happy that her self-termed 'hobby' of prison reform had re-entered her life. The female prisoners experienced vermin-infected combs, cruelty from the prison officers and drinking water contaminated with brick dust. From this time onwards, these prominent Suffragettes became Con's friends, and she began to write about them with reverence and comradely recognition.

Since Con had been a teenager, she had always displayed signs of a readiness to give herself completely towards good causes. Letters from 1892 between Con and her sister Betty include Con declaring, 'what a mistake it is to care only for little things, or to care for things only a little,' and maintaining 'if one only cares enough, there is strength enough to overcome every obstacle, or at least to endure every martyrdom'. To Con, the Suffragettes became a cause that was worth 'caring enough' about and they confirmed her beliefs that life as an unmarried upper-class woman had no great purpose and was cluttered with 'little things' that made no sense to care about. She later wrote in her book, *Prisons and Prisoners*, that 'I myself was one of that numerous gang of upper-class leisured spinsters for whom a maiming subserviency is so conditional to their very existence that it becomes an aim in itself.' Much of her excessive hyperbole written in her memoirs was aimed at those lower-class Suffragettes who overlooked or did not understand some of the restrictions applied to the upper-class women like Con, for instance:

To the single women, the old maid of later years, the paralysing worship of incapacity dominates life, the chain of limitations and restrictions is but seldom broken, and never overcome save by exceptional force of character or ability. Even then how often it is only the beating of wings against unyielding and maiming bars.

Annie Kenney described meeting Con at Littlehampton in her book *Memories of a Militant*:

Tall, majestic, noble to me she looked what she was – one of England's great noblewomen…She always wore long flowing scarves which reminded me of a bunch of lavender enveloped by clouds of delicate, varied hues. Her voice was quiet with a depth of feeling and, to me, a touch of sadness.

Annie suggested that Con was very curious about the Suffragettes' behaviour: 'She had wanted to know the why and wherefore of every move we had made…she was one of those who desired to know the truth of why certain actions had been taken.'

In a letter to Adela Smith on 10 September, Con described the experiences she had had on her holiday:

Letters to you have buzzed in my brain and throbbed in my heart, but you know how time behaves when one is taking a plunge into new surroundings, new friends, new interests... Telegraphically this is my latest:- Got knotted up with Suffragettes down at the club in Littlehampton; through them have come into personal first-hand contact with prison abuses. The hobby of prison reform has thereby taken on new vigour, and intends to cut its first teeth [in me] via an interview with Ruggles-Brise, and an interview with the female inspector of Holloway prison [Dr Mary Gordon], and taking part in the Suffragette breakfast to the next batch of released Suffrage prisoners on September 16...After sending you that wee line about Mrs Pethick Lawrence as a friend of Olive Schreiner, I had a long talk-out with her in a motor expedition. She mostly talked Woman Suffrage, about which, though I sympathise with the cause, she left me uncoverted as to my criticisms of some of their methods...Mrs Lawrence is an entirely lovable and sympathetic woman of the Olive Schreiner type.

The second chapter in *Prisons and Prisoners*, entitled 'My Conversion', explains how, after Con became aware of Emmeline Pethick-Lawrence and Annie Kenney's militant allegiances, she told the pair that although she 'shared their wish for the enfranchisement of women,' she did not 'at all sympathise with all the measures they adopted for bringing about that reform'. However, Con later had an epiphany whilst walking through Littlehampton, which led her to compare the treatment of sheep to women:

But on seeing this sheep it seemed to reveal to me for the first time the position of women throughout the world. I realised how often women are held in contempt as beings outside the pale of human dignity...I was ashamed to remember that...I had been blind to the sufferings peculiar to women as such.

It took Con six weeks to read and extensively study the question of the enfranchisement of women. She subscribed to *Votes for Women* (the WSPU newspaper), and after that became a whole-hearted Suffragette. Con loved reading about social and legal reforms. When contemplating these issues, she would see 'whether or not the women alive today in the working class could be cured is of comparatively little importance' and then added later in *Prisons and Prisoners* that 'clearly the causes which have brought them forth must not be altered at the root,' perhaps referring to the possibility at that time of the vote being given only to women of certain means. Con had also made an impression with the leading Suffragettes, perhaps because she was a 'lady' and the cause was looking to add upper-class names to their list of supporters.

The WSPU was to fill an emotional void left by the unhappy love affair with John Ponsonby, after her hopes had been left dashed when he announced he had found someone else. But Con's other attraction to the WSPU was that she was nearly 40 years of age and clearly felt that she needed a purpose in life, other than caring for her mother and supervising her nieces and nephews. By being a member of such an organisation, and taking part in their more militant activities, there was always a distinct possibility that she might go to prison and therefore help towards the cause of prison reform, which she felt as keenly about as the prevention of cruelty to animals. Con had written letters to MPs regarding prison conditions following discussions from released female prisoners and in turn received letters stating that the conditions were not as bad as described.

Despite not always enjoying the best of health, Con felt that within the Suffragettes she might still be able to aid the most desperate and weak. When she joined the WSPU, Con was able to transfer her feelings of needing to help others to the leadership of the cause, having spent a lifetime trying to please her family. The WSPU was to lift her out of the deep depression she had found herself in where she was experiencing the sense of being unloved and unlovable. For example, when talking about the overwhelming feelings of the rejection by Ponsonby, she used the imagery of hunger and thirst to describe how she felt: 'And I yearn and thirst, Oh! Such thirst, for unattainable life fillers to be in my life.'

In *Memories of a Militant*, Annie Kenney said of Con that 'it was a joy talking to her. She was so understanding and sympathetic even in her opposition. After her conversion [to the Suffragettes] she was one of the finest, most unselfish and most loyal of loyalists.' Annie also added 'Her passion and devotion for the working-class women in the Movement was quite out of the ordinary. She loved them and they loved her. She was one of the few people in the world that sees in others nothing but good.' For the leaders of the WSPU, 'Only those at the head realised the tremendous asset it was for the Movement when Lady Constance Lytton, a member of one of England's most illustrious families, joined us.'

Was Con's life as much of an act as Jane Warton (the person Con later morphed into) was? There was thought to be a similar movement throughout her life where she went against the idea of being a member of a family who had an obvious display of aristocracy, personified by imperialism and wealth. Was her act of joining the Suffragettes merely a rebellion against her family?

It would seem, however, that Con's interest in suffrage did not suddenly develop as a result of her visit to Littlehampton. Indeed, her family had some links to campaign groups and interestingly, Con's sisters Betty and Emily claimed to have been the first to have peaked Con's interest in women's suffrage. Betty's sister-in-law, Lady Frances Balfour, was involved with the Conservative and Unionist Women's Suffrage Association and was the President of the London Society for Women's Suffrage. The tactics used by these associations preferred more constitutional routes towards reform rather than the militant tactics used by the Pankhurst-led union, the WSPU, who opted for deeds over words.

Con was not the only member of the WSPU who came from an affluent background. Emmeline and Frederick Pethick-Lawrence, for example, were a wealthy left-wing couple. With their connections and associated resources, they widened the class base of the WSPU showing that the group represented no single class or party, particularly as Emmeline became treasurer of the WSPU. The secretary of the union's Manchester branch, Alice Milne, attended a London meeting and recorded to her delight that the event was 'full of fashionable ladies in rustling silks and satins' and that the WSPU took every possible opportunity to show both the public and the government that it had a diverse membership. Annie Kenney described how 'thousands upon thousands joined us. Women of every profession and trade and occupation had thrown in their lot with ours...aristocracy was represented by Lady Constance Lytton; poor democracy by Mrs Sparborough.'

Clements Inn, just north of the Strand, was the home of the Pethick-Lawrences. Founders and editors of *Votes for Women*, the couple allowed their home to become the headquarters of the WSPU between 1907 and 1912, occupying a grand total of twenty-seven rooms, before the organisation moved around the corner to Kingsway. Caxton Hall, the venue for the WSPU's 'Women's Parliaments' and the base for organising deputations, was located in Westminster, near to the government offices and the Houses of Parliament. Ethel Smyth described Frederick Pethick-Lawrence in *Female Pipings in Eden*, as 'the wonderful Mr Pethick-Lawrence, who was ever ready to take root in any police station, his money bag between his feet, at any hour of the day or night'.

Gradually, Con came to accept the Suffragettes' militant tactics, even though she had previously believed that the physical acts of violence they were becoming known for were unnecessary. She came to serve as a movement lecturer and agitator for the WSPU for four years, despite her delicate health and her intense dislike of being in the public eye, much preferring instead to lurk in the shadows whenever possible.

Con would later become aware that back in July 1908, the Home Secretary, Herbert Gladstone, allowed all women who were imprisoned in Holloway and who were connected with the recent Suffragette disturbances, to be allowed to use a notebook and pencil if they so wished. These writing materials, used for making notes, letters or journals, could be kept within their cells and there was no need for them to be examined by the staff unless the Commissioners wished to do so. This would apply to all women in the second division and to women in the third division currently. The second-division prisoners were regarded as criminals. Treated like ordinary prisoners, they were locked up in separate cells, wore a prison uniform of green serge dresses and faced a harsh prison regime. Prisoners in the third division, meanwhile, as well as experiencing the second-division conditions, also carried out hard manual labour and were recognisable by their brown dresses.

In addition to the political differences regarding the treatment of prisoners, a letter written in July 1908 by Herbert Nield MP discussing the conditions of the women in Holloway, and which was later mentioned in a biography of Christabel Pankhurst, would become a popular topic of discussion by Con. The letter referred to two distinct questions; firstly, that perhaps there should be a contrast between political and criminal prisoners, and secondly, that maybe the conditions of the prisoners within the second division should be improved. In regards to the first question, Nield suggested that political offences hardly existed in Britain and that only those prisoners who were convicted of seditious libel and sedition, and those possibly who were convicted of treason, were to be remanded as prisoners of the first division, but any offences against public peace, property and persons, whether or not done for political purposes, were subject to the normal laws. He suggested that it would be impossible to differentiate between crimes as to whether they had a political motive and, as such, the existing laws worked well in the courts. He went on to say that the prisoners to whom the letter referred knew that they had to face the consequences of their actions in order to attract public attraction. Nield was not in favour of the prison system as it currently stood and despite some reform having occurred, and him having devoted time in reform legislation, more needed to be done. The letter concluded with a short paragraph in which Nield addressed the second question: the conditions of the second division. Here, Mr Nield felt that the treatment of the second-division prisoners was too close to the third division and that he was considering how best to improve the situation. However, nothing in the form of prison reform really changed for Con and the rest of the Suffragettes at this time.

In September 1908, Betty Balfour wrote a letter to Gladstone, enclosing within it part of a letter written by her sister Con that Gerald, Betty's husband, thought the Home Secretary might want to see. She stated that Con had been meeting Mrs Pankhurst in Littlehampton and had gathered some important details about the suffrage movement. Con had referred to Mrs Pankhurst as 'soft & womanish & charmful', finding her to have an excellent voice and manners, and a great intellect. She went on to say that Mrs Pankhurst had travelled a great deal and that she had learnt Arabic in a matter of weeks. Betty added that she had heard of a Suffragette plot and believed that they were planning to kidnap someone and keep them captive until the Prime Minister met their demands.

Emmeline Pankhurst, the leader of the WSPU, described the importance of women's suffrage in a small publication simply entitled *The Importance of the Vote*, which was designed to appeal to women, like Con, who were warming to the idea of women having the vote:

> First of all, a symbol, secondly, a safeguard, and thirdly, an instrument. It is a symbol of freedom, a symbol of citizenship, a symbol of liberty. It is a safeguard of all those liberties which it symbolises. And in the later days it has come to be regarded more than anything else as an instrument, something

with which you can get a great many more things than our forefathers who fought for the vote ever realised as possible to get with it.

On 13 October, Parliament reopened after recess, as did the Women's Parliament the WSPU had been holding. A handbill was issued that broadcast an advertisement stating 'Men and Women, HELP THE SUFFRAGETTES TO RUSH THE HOUSES OF PARLIAMENT'. A Votes for Women kite was floated over the House of Commons and a steamer was launched to patrol the river Thames with posters announcing the forthcoming demonstration.

At a crowded meeting at the Queen's Hall on the previous day, 12 October, Con was in the audience when it was announced that Christabel and Emmeline Pankhurst and Flora Drummond were expecting to be arrested at any moment on the platform. At midday, a summons for the trio to appear at Bow Street that afternoon had been served upon the leaders in relation to the 'rush' handbill. The leaders had instead ignored the summons and had proceeded to their meeting at the Queen's Hall, where suspense and excitement were running high throughout the crowd that had gathered to listen to the meeting. However, a message soon came through that the magistrate, Curtis Bennett, had adjourned the summonses until the next morning. The excitement was further enhanced as the trio again declined to appear at their summonses and instead sent a message to the court to say that they would not be in attendance at their offices until 6 pm the next day, 'When we shall all three be entirely at your disposal'. The magistrate was then forced to issue a warrant for their arrest, but the police were somehow unable to execute it until the appointed hour given in the note, when the three appeared at their office and were taken immediately to the cells at Bow Street.

Con's important role within the WSPU began when she offered herself as another assistant to the cause for Mrs Pethick-Lawrence and the Suffragettes, and her conversation with one of the main members of the WSPU was retold in a letter to her mother:

> You know my reservations as to some of your methods, my sympathies are much more with you than with any of your opponents, but it is no good volunteering to form part of your deputations, to sit on your platforms, etc. I should have to publicly state my disagreement with part of your tactics, and you would feel me a traitor in the Camp. But of course I want to be of use if I can. Is there anything I can possibly do to help you?

Con continued to describe the talk she had shared with Mrs Pethick Lawrence, who had agreed that Con could help the WSPU in their cause. She suggested that Con contact Herbert Gladstone to persuade him to rethink the treatment of Suffragettes, who were being treated as 'common criminals' rather than 'political offenders'.

Con went on to describe her day in the same letter to her mother, relating how she was 'incessantly on the move', as she put it, from about 4 pm to 11.30 that night, shuttling between Clements Inn, the Houses of Parliament, the private residence of the magistrate and Bow Street Police Station. She later retold in her book *Prisons and Prisoners* that she was able to view the crowd that had been drawn by the infamous handbill and was able to study the 'attitude of mind' of the Home Office, the authorities, and the police towards the women's movement. However, at this point Con had still not fully committed to joining the WSPU, and still believed she needed to convince her mother that it was a worthwhile cause, without worrying about potentially disappointing her family.

Con felt that 'the decisions of the government were predetermined and detached from any consideration of the political demand which was the root cause of the women's rebellion.' The deputation had still gone ahead, led by Marion Wallace Dunlop, and around 60,000 people had gathered in attendance, requiring the police to cordon off Parliament Square after the situation was reported to have been chaotic and violent. The immense crowd contained people with a variety of different opinions on the subject of women's suffrage, with some being enthusiastically in favour, while others displayed angry hostility. It included men and women of all classes, although the women showed no enthusiasm for hooliganism.

Con's first objective was to obtain an interview with Home Secretary Herbert Gladstone at the House of Commons. Unfortunately, she was not able to see him but found a friendly Member of Parliament who was willing to act as a messenger between the two of them. Their exchange went as follows:

Question: Would he [Gladstone] use his powers to ensure that the three prisoners [Christabel Pankhurst, Emmeline Pankhurst and Flora Drummond] should be sentenced to the first division and not to the second division, as if they were common criminals, which obviously they were not?

Reply: As the prisoners were not yet arrested, he could not possibly adjudicate on the question of their sentences.

Question: If I [Con] returned at 6 o'clock, the hour when they were to surrender to the summons, would he then give me an answer?

Reply: He had not the power, the question rested with the police-court authorities; he had determined never to interfere with sentences.

Question: Would he give me a permit or some sort of facilities to approach the magistrate?

Her messenger imparted that it would be no good putting this question to Mr Gladstone as he was already angry regarding the proceedings, and that even if the Home Secretary had the power, he would not be induced to help the Suffragettes receive first division treatment.

Con then headed to the Bow Street Police Station. She found that on her way the crowds were dense at Parliament Square, Parliament Street and Trafalgar Square, and by the time she reached Bow Street, it was past 6 pm and the magistrate she wished to see had already left to go home. The superintendent Con saw at the station was not wearing the usual policeman's helmet but a flat cap and was very civil to her. He said it was against the rules to give out the private addresses of magistrates and that the one she wished to see, Mr Curtis Bennett, would not return until 10 am the following morning when court resumed. However, the superintendent was helpful, adding, 'The prisoners are here now, in the cells, would you like to see them?' Feeling 'almost overwhelmed that so unworthy and half-hearted a follower as myself should be the one to have this grand opportunity,' Con, 'availed [herself] of it without a moment's hesitation.' She was shown through the building along a series of passages and then up a flight of stairs to where a wardress was in charge. She described in her book how the air became cold and damp and she realised the meaning of the word 'puanteur', which was used by Dostoevsky in his descriptions of his own imprisonment. Con recounted how the smell of deadness pervaded the building, which was used to incarcerate human beings solely for punitive measures.

The wardress asked which of the three prisoners Con wished to see and she decided upon Mrs Emmeline Pankhurst. Con described the cells as horse boxes within a stable that had a small grating on each. Inside, these boxes closely resembled an animal's den; poorly lit with just a wooden bench and a sanitary convenience. Con recalled seeing 'a woman whose appearance struck awe into every fibre of my being' standing erect and moving towards the grating. Pankhurst herself appeared to be defiant and indignant but remained controlled. Con wrote:

> From that moment I recognised in her, and I have held the vision undimmed ever since, the guardian protector of this amazing woman's movement, conscious not only of the thousands who follow her lead today, but of the martyred generations of the past and of the women of the future whose welfare depend upon the path hewn out for them today.

She saw Mrs Pankhurst as a pioneer who shirked none of the responsibilities required of her and compared her to an arrowhead deriving its force from the construction of the whole weapon.

Upon talking to the lady in question, Con was advised by Mrs Pankhurst how best to use her proffered services and not to worry about the situation of not being held as first division prisoners; the prisoners themselves could plead this when they came up before the court. The most important thing, said Mrs Pankhurst, was to try to get the ladies released for the night or they would not be able to plead properly the following day due to fatigue.

Con searched for the magistrate in the 'wilds of West Kensington', as she called it, and thus returned again to Clements Inn. She eventually tracked down her quarry near Olympia, where the magistrate Mr Curtis Bennett received her courteously but was said to have adopted a defensive expression upon learning about her reason for calling. Mr Bennett said he could make no comment as to which division he would sentence the prisoners and nor could the prisoners be let out on bail as the ladies had responded to their summonses at such a late hour. However, in regard to taking food and bedding to the ladies, that would be down to the police to decide as it was beyond his jurisdiction.

Con returned to Mrs Pethick-Lawrence at Clements Inn and they quickly gathered together bedding, cushions and rugs before heading off to the police station at Bow Street at the very late hour of 11 pm. Upon arrival they discovered that they had been beaten to it by James Murray, the Liberal MP for East Aberdeenshire, who had visited the prisoners in question and ordered several items from the Savoy Hotel to make them comfortable for the night. In addition, an elaborate meal was served by three waiters in the prison superintendent's room, which was brightened by tall wax candles, silver, flowers and bonbons.

The trial was due to take place the following day, but Christabel Pankhurst asked for an adjournment to take legal advice and to prepare a defence. Her request was successful and the trial was adjourned for a week. Con said that it was thanks to Mrs Pankhurst's speech at the subsequent trial that she felt she had been taken hold of by the movement, declaring 'every sentence of it seemed to be true, dignified, strong, entirely respectful.' The passage that seemed to have the greatest effect was as follows:

> You know that women have tried to do something to come to the aid of their own sex...I was in the hospital at Holloway, and when I was there I heard from one of the beds near me the moans of a woman who was in the pangs of childbirth. I should like you to realise how women feel at helpless little infants breathing their first breath in the atmosphere of a prison. We believe if we get the vote, we will find some more humane way of dealing with women than that.

Flora Drummond also made Con feel faith in the women's movement and Christabel Pankhurst was the sunrise of that cause. It seemed to Con and other followers of the WSPU that a kind of darkness had fallen when the three ladies were in prison, despite Mrs Pethick-Lawrence and Sylvia Pankhurst, Christabel's sister, keeping the meetings going at the Queen's Hall. Con wrote in *Prisons and*

Prisoners: 'I needed no converting now and my only wish was to convince my mother.'

Con's transformation was difficult for the family; she talked incessantly about 'the Cause' and her family found it boring, fearing she had become radicalised into a socialist movement. Con was described by a member of the family, Judith Blunt (Neville's wife), as lost to her mother forever: 'just as a tame hawk which has shaken off its hood and flown away into the sky.' Her family had been shaken by her decision to join the Suffragettes; they had a conventional attitude towards politics and reforms and Edith particularly disliked the militant Suffragettes and was upset at their influence over her daughter. She also feared for Con's health and knew that it would not withstand the militancy used by other Suffragettes. In a letter sent to Con on 28 November 1908, Edith said:

> Darling, I am so thankful for your letter telling me you are better. You don't realise one bit what I feel of real misery at the work of your leaders, which I feel is really wicked and wrong, and leading to murder being done as a noble duty, which is against all my principles and beliefs, and I see it is all spoiling my beloved perfect child. So I can never go to any meetings where the leaders are, or where their principles are being praised. I am very sorry Vic is taking the chair at the City Meeting, but he hopes to do good, which I fear he cannot.

Aunt T was also becoming disinterested with the cause. Having previously refused to sign a paper backing women's suffrage, Con had written to her expressing disappointment. Aunt T was also saddened to have lost Con to the Suffragettes, as can be seen in letters reproduced in Betty Balfour's *Letters of Constance Lytton*. Aunt T made no secret that she now found the campaign boring and was baffled that Con was interested in it. 'The difference between you and me over the suffrage question,' lamented Con, 'is that you think votes for females desirable but not important.' She then went on to suggest that Aunt T should attend one of the suffrage meetings to fully understand the current situation.

In a letter to Adela Smith from October 1908, Con wrote, 'Apparently my name is in the *Daily Mail* of today and poor Mother hugely upset about it.' To her mother, Edith, she said:

> It is wretched that you are distressed and unhappy because of me. I have not seen the *Daily Mail*, don't know what it says. Of course I did not give my name to any press man, nor make a bid for publicity. I have done nothing that you need be ashamed of. I have refused to do several things I should like to do, and would do, but for you. Will you at least trust me not to do anything contrary to my nature, to my opinions, and to my upbringing? I know that lots of things I do you think wild and unnecessary, but do you honestly think I have up till now done anything which you seriously consider a disgrace? Wild things are like me; I shall probably do them again. Think and believe the worst of me in this respect. But until you know the facts, don't believe from rumour that I have done anything which I too should think disgraceful. Devoted, always most miserable to grieve you.

Meanwhile, Betty Balfour, writing in *Letters of Constance Lytton* said that:

> Her [Con's] brother, Lord Lytton, did not fail her as a staunch and loyal friend. He not only believed in her cause but was prepared to work for it in every way consistent with his own views of what was right. He defended Con's quixotic actions to her mother, and lessened her pain by his sympathy.

Olive Schreiner, writing to her sister-in-law Fan (Frances) Schreiner, declared, 'Did I tell you that my dear friend Lady Constance Lytton has become a great suffragette? & the wonderful thing is that she has got old Lady Lytton quite to sympathise with her, who is very conservative even more so than Lady Loch!'

Writing from Homewood in late December 1908, Con sent a short letter to Mr Gladstone, wanting him to know how much happiness he had caused by the unexpected premature release of the Suffragette prisoners. She had visited the Suffrage Women's Headquarters at Clements Inn and witnessed an unusual sight: much happiness 'bubbling in the air' and the rooms very much alive with joy at the thought of seeing Mrs Pankhurst and the other imprisoned ladies very soon. She feared that Mr Gladstone may consider her to have 'Suffragette impudence' as she had found courage within herself to write to him personally to thank him for his gesture at releasing the prisoners early for Christmas.

Con described to Aunt T her new-found devotion to the suffrage movement, writing:

> I go deeper and deeper in my enthusiasm for the women, and even for their 'tactics' as I understand it more and more, – not only what they do, but what has been done to them to drive them to these tactics. I feel the Government opened the ball, not they, but of course once they have been aroused, these exasperations on the part of the cause-fighters are always difficult to deal with…I send you Mrs Humphrey Ward's pamphlets as well as the others. If you have any lurking unsympathy for the suffragettes, I think she will help dispel it.

Chapter 4

Early Prison Years, 1909

On 19 January 1909, Con officially joined the WSPU and offered herself to Mrs Pethick-Lawrence for the next deputation. Writing later in *Prisons and Prisoners*, Con said that 'Women had tried repeatedly, and always in vain, every peaceable means open to them of influencing successive governments. Processions and petitions were absolutely useless. In January 1909 I decided to become a member of the WSPU.'

On 24 February Con participated in her first deputation and also experienced her first arrest. On the same day, one of the regular meetings of the Women's Parliament was held in Caxton Hall. Sylvia Pankhurst described in her book *The Suffragette* how Mrs Pethick-Lawrence sallied forth from the meeting with a number of women in her train. However, she and twenty-eight of her comrades, including Miss Daisy Solomon (the daughter of the late Prime Minister of the Cape), Caprina Fahey (daughter of the sculptor Albert Gilbert) and Con were soon arrested for attempting to reach the House of Commons. Those who were recognised by the police as leaders were quickly taken into custody; the other protestors were said to have been treated with great violence, with the constables seizing and hurling them bodily back into the crowd. One woman sprained her ankle, while another had a thumb dislocated. However, the Suffragettes maintained their stoic policy and made no complaints against the actions of the police. Con wrote of this event that 'The word went around that we were to conceal as best we might our various injuries.

It was no part of our policy to get the police into trouble...The most difficult thing to disguise was the wounded nose of Miss Dugdale.'

From the start of the Suffragette activities up to the outbreak of the First World War, over 1,000 women were sent to prison because of their suffrage actions. The vast majority of these were WSPU members.

On 26 February 1909, the *Belfast News Letter* reported that Con had been bound over as part of a group of Suffragettes who had appeared at Bow Street. Mrs Pethick-Lawrence, one of the defendants, had read out a long statement in court 'Declaring that they had broken a technical law, but no moral or Constitutional law, as they had a right to present a petition to Parliament.' Con had said that she had voluntarily asked if she was allowed to help the women's cause and had never been prouder in her life. She refused to promise not to try to force her way into the House again and as such the magistrate had to bound her over for £30, or one-month's imprisonment. Sentences of a similar nature were given to twenty-four other women, including Una Stratford Dugdale (the daughter of Commander Dugdale) and Mrs Ellen Kirkpatrick Watte of Lenton, Nottinghamshire. The *Dundee Courier* also carried a similar headline declaring 'Lady Constance Lytton will spend a month in prison'.

On the following day, the *Londonderry Sentinel* wrote that there was a large gathering at Bow Street Police Court in connection with the police raid the previous night at Westminster. The first defendants to come before Sir Alfred Rutzen were Mrs Pethick-Lawrence and Leslie Lawson, who were both charged with obstruction. Inspector Jarvis mentioned that the defendants had asked to see Mr Asquith, the Prime Minister, and he had told them that Mr Asquith was not present in the House. The ladies did not accept his offer to take in their resolution and had said that they must go in. They then persisted in their attempt to pass the police blockade and a great struggle had taken place between the ladies and the police, with these two defendants being particularly prominent in their attempts. Due to the 'state of affairs' the police reserve had to be called.

Members of the Suffragettes before the dock at the court were: Catherine Tyson of Streatham; Muriel Roberts of Hampstead; Daisy Dorothea Solomon; Kate Waishe, from Pentonville; Evelyn Cheshire, from Ealing; Ellen Kirkpatrick Watts of Lenton; Mrs Caprina Fahey; Margaret Davis Colley of Pulborough, Sussex; Mrs Sarah Carwin; Mrs Rose Yates (who protested against receiving second-division treatment); Elen Wines Pitman; Annie Ainsworth; Marie Freeman (who apparently smiled in court); Katherine Richmond; Margaret Eleanor Thompson; Madeline Petre; Helen Tyson; Catherine Isabel Ida Corbett; Una Dugdale of Stanhope Place; Catherine Townsend; Margaret Rogers; Mary Allen of Winterbury, Bristol; and Leslie Lawson, who was originally sentenced to two months' imprisonment but was brought back into the courtroom and her sentence reduced down to one month, although she protested against the reduction. Elsa Gye of Fulham was given six weeks' imprisonment, while Thomas Mortimer Budgett – the only man to be charged and who is said to have declared that 'the women are not going to do all the dirty work' – was given one month's imprisonment. Una Dugdale stated that she wished to protest against the inhuman and brutal treatment that had been handed out to the women on behalf of the Liberal government, adding that she thought there was a 'higher, divine justice' which would bring Mr Asquith and his colleagues to account for their cruelty to women for asking for their enfranchisement.

When Con stood in the Bow Street Magistrates Court awaiting her sentence for her first stint in Holloway prison, she described it as being the proudest she had ever felt about anything in her life. Christabel Pankhurst even thanked her afterwards for her contribution, which was an unlooked for honour.

Con envisaged the Black Maria that carried her to Holloway as a hearse that was bearing coffins to their graves and as such was transporting her to the underworld. When she entered the vehicle, she felt that she was about to start the journey to a living death. One wonders if she felt like a martyr for the Suffragette cause, desperate to escape the matriarchal restrictions placed upon her, with prison offering some well-earned freedom.

Upon arriving at the prison, Con was stunned to find herself in the prison hospital rather than a cell. She was determined to prove to the prison authorities that she could endure the conditions of the punishment cell, so she slept on the floor on a mattress rather than the hospital bed. When she was finally given what she asked for, the four walls of her own cell, she later wrote of her delight that 'at last the longed-for moment had arrived'.

In a letter to her mother written on 24 February 1909 and later printed in *Prisons and Prisoners,* Con described how her concern for women prisoners was a form of maternal desire, her 'hobby' as she called it:

> What maternity there lurks in me has for years past been gradually awakening over the prisoners, the deliberate, cruel harm that is done to them, their souls and their bodies, the ignorant exasperating waste of good opportunities in connection with them till now the thought of them, the yearning after them, turns in me and tugs at me as vitally and irrepressibly as ever a physical child can call upon its mother. The moment I got near the suffragettes the way to this child of mine seemed easy and straight.

It is perhaps useful here to describe the typical prison conditions Con would have endured during her stay at Holloway. On entry, any prisoners would have immediately been told to be silent by the wardresses. At first the women would have been locked into reception cells before being sent to see the doctors for an initial examination. After that, the prisoners were searched to ensure that they were not concealing any illegal items before being ordered to undress. Their clothes were stored by the prison authorities, and they were ordered to give details about their name, address, profession, age, and religion, and also whether each woman could sew, read or write. The prisoners were then ordered to take a bath, although each individual bath was separated from the next by a partition so that the wardresses could still observe each bather carrying out their private wash. After drying off, the prisoners had to put on the prison uniform from the piles on the floor. Third-class prisoners wore brown dresses and second-class green serge dresses. All prisoners alike wore blue and white checked aprons, white caps, and were given a big blue and white handkerchief, which was to last a week. The underclothing was coarse and poorly fitted, not to mention the big clumpy shoes the women had to wear. Stockings, black in colour with red stripes, came without garters or suspenders to keep them up. All items were branded and each prisoner was given a yellow badge bearing the letter of her block and the number of her cell; this would be what the prisoner was known by until her release.

The prison routine would have started with a waking up bell at around 5.30 am. Breakfast, served at 7.15, would have consisted of a pint of sweet tea, while a small brown loaf and two ounces of butter (to last all day) was given to the prisoner in her own cell. Prior to attending chapel, the prisoner needed to scrub her floor and the three planks forming her bedstead, empty her slops, fold up the bedclothes into a roll and stow these away along with the mattress and pillow. Her utensils also had to be polished with soap and bath brick (the former version of a scouring pad and of a similar size to a house brick). The cell was then inspected to check that these tasks were completed in the required manner. Church and an hour of exercise were undertaken with no talking before lunch at 12. Supper was taken at 5 pm, which consisted of a small loaf and a pint of cocoa, accompanied by a thick layer of grease on top. Each cell had an electric light which was controlled externally and was turned off at 8 pm every night.

Each prisoner spent the first four weeks of their imprisonment mostly in their cell and during this time they would undertake associated labour, such as knitting men's socks or making nightgowns. Luxuries such as a bath could be taken once a week, and books could be borrowed from the very basic prison library twice a week. After the month expired, prisoners were allowed to bring their needlework or knitting to the hall and sit side by side silently. Anyone who was serving one month in the second division was forbidden to communicate with the outside world through any means.

One of the reasons that Con became famous as a Suffragette, other than for her class and for writing *Prisons and Prisoners*, is that she attempted to mutilate her body for the cause. Unfortunately for her, her plan was detected by the authorities when she asked for dressings to avoid blood poisoning. In *Prisons and Prisoners* she wrote:

> I had decided to write the words 'Votes for Women' on my body, scratching it on my skin with a needle, beginning over the heart and ending on my face. I proposed to show the first half of the inscription to doctors, telling them that, as I know how much appearances were respected by officials. I thought it well to warn that the last letter and a full stop would come upon my cheek and be quite fresh and visible on the day of my release.

However, Con found her skin to be tougher than she expected. She had first attempted her plan with a sewing needle and when that failed, a darning needle, before finally using a piece of sharpened enamel. It took twenty minutes just to carve out the V on her breast, but she felt it looked deeper than she had originally intended and as such sought out help from a prison officer.

Early Prison Years, 1909

I felt all a craftsman's satisfaction in my job. The V was very clearly and evenly printed in spite of the varying material of its background, a rib bone forming an awkward bump. As I pointed out to the doctor, it had been placed exactly over the heart and visibly recorded the pulsation of that organ as clearly as a watch hand, so that he no longer needed to be put to the trouble of a stethoscope.

Her self-esteem having been much reduced in the past, an exhibitionist act such as this must have been extremely liberating and empowering.

Con also worsened the conditions of her prison cell, forcing open the windows, despite the winter conditions outside. This was part of the political action endorsed by the WSPU, whereby prisoners would break open the windows by using their shoes. In contrast, when at home, Con would feel the cold easily and frequently kept herself warm by polishing her shoes rather than lighting a fire.

Despite being in prison, Con was always finding opportunities in which she could serve. She assisted the prison hospital cleaners, waited on the sick prisoners and even rubbed the chest of a prison wardress who was suffering from a bad cough. She refused many enrichments offered to her because these same options were not offered to her fellow prison companions. Con was always profuse in expressing admiration for her Suffragette comrades and was said by Betty to have 'laid equal emphasis on the kindness and care of her relatives on the illnesses consequent on her suffrage work and imprisonments.'

Using a slate pencil and soap mixed with dirt from the floor for ink, Con wrote on the wall of her prison cell, 'Under a government which imprisons any unjustly, the true place for a just man (or woman) is also a prison.' The quote itself was from an essay about civil disobedience by the ex-prisoner Henry Thoreau.

While in prison, one of the most painful moments for Con was being forced to choose between daughterly affection, between her and her mother, and the solidarity she felt between her and her 'sisters', the Suffragettes. She received letters from her mother, even though prison rules normally did not allow inmates to read their letters. Con did not want to be given special privileges because she was of a different social class but instead wanted to be treated the same as the other prisoners.

Con was also perturbed by the noises coming from the rest of the prison. The way it sounded like these other women were being treated seemed very irrational in the extreme to Con. She later found out that the shrieks she had heard in her prison cell were of an insane woman who was under remand. Con had thought that the days when the cruel treatment of mentally deficient people was considered reasonable or justifiable had passed, and that the woman in a cell below her should not have been alone, regardless of whether she was sane or insane. Con wrote to Gladstone after her release that she did not think the prison officials relayed the truthful information to the government. Gladstone wrote a pleasing letter back and Con at this time thought that he might be on her side regarding reforms. She suggested to him that the amendment regarding the death sentence that was moved by the Lord Chancellor and unwisely rejected by the House of Lords after the Daisy Lord case should be considered again to avoid the 'frequent enactment' of what many people considered a 'ghastly and inhuman process'.

The case Con referred to here concerned Daisy Lord, a young woman who had been given a life sentence for killing her young baby 'whilst in a paroxysm of terror at the thought of its future'. Daisy Lord was later reprieved to penal servitude before her sentence was reduced to one year, ten months and twenty-four days. Con had said to Mr Gladstone that she wished the true facts could be made available to prisoners instead of letting them believe that they were to be hanged, and 'that the government members should realise the state of mind, body & soul induced on these women who had already been in much anguish and misery which had led them to the stage that they were now at.'

Later, after her release, on 4 April Con wrote to Mr Gladstone again saying how pleased she was that he had taken the trouble to reply to her earlier letter. She asked to meet him in a private capacity to listen to his views on prison reform, and to offer up her own short and limited experience of prison. She described her views on infanticide cases, seeing such crimes as serious as criminal ones, but which also affected the welfare of the community, should women be imprisoned for mental illness such as postnatal depression.

There was an impression, with some people, that Con condoned child murder via her speeches, as she discussed with her sister Betty Balfour:

My hearer seems to have concluded that I commended child murder. Whenever I have mentioned that prison yarn, this has been my line: got to know a woman with a good sympathetic face and ways…She had killed her own child. But when I came to learn the conditions of extreme physical misery, of appalling moral degradation, under which she had committed that act, I felt I should have done the same myself. The workhouse would have been no solution; it is simply a form of social suicide. She had one child already, to whom she was devoted, which she had supported entirely as well as herself…

Con's feelings were very strong in regard to punitive measures, which seemed harmful and injudicious to her. She reiterated that she was not concerned with the sentimental aspect of prison reform but with the folly of penalising an already twisted woman before sending her back to her wretched lifestyle and existence, where she would probably have more children who would endure the same suffering. Con spoke further about her comments regarding the shrieking mad woman she had mentioned previously, saying she felt that nothing was done to allay the distress that the woman was suffering. Con was not complaining about the wardress perse, but how the wardress' 'dispositions were not tainted by the regulations that were in place'.

Prior to Con's release, she had written to her brother Victor and told him how Mrs Pethick-Lawrence had heard from her husband that when the twenty-six of their deputation (and Thomas Mortimer Budgett, the man who had been imprisoned alongside them), were to be released on 24 March, the plan would be to meet up outside the prison, as usual, and then there would be an evening feast instead of the regular breakfast affair to celebrate the prisoners' release. Although she appreciated the gesture, she felt it would be inconvenient to a lot of the ladies concerned, including herself, and preferred the informality of the breakfasts where she felt she could offer one or two bits of her mind in comparison to the speeches expected at a dinner. She also believed that she had a prior engagement at Aunt T's Liberal League Meeting in Surrey. However, upon their release, the ladies were nevertheless entertained to a dinner in the evening, at which Con gave a speech, although she said she did not wish to pose as a martyr because her heart condition meant she was not allowed to scrub her own floor in the prison.

Betty Balfour wrote of Con's release, 'I and two of my children went to greet her at the doors of the prison on her release on March 24. As soon as I saw her, I realised as I had not done before that she no longer belonged to us. She belonged to her union, and nothing else really counted.' These thoughts were also repeated in a letter between Emily and Aunt T:

> I must write you a line of deepest sympathy...we cannot disguise from ourselves that our old Con has gone forever. I feel, whatever it may be in the future, for the moment she has passed out of the lives of her family, except in so far as they

can go with her into the new life and interest. I think she has ceased to have any private affection even. She has become an impersonal being, and no one will feel this so much as you.

But from Con's point of view, she felt she had just given more of her love and expanded her family; she did not love or care for any members of her original family any less.

To Con's distress, one of the Freedom League Members, Mrs Meredith MacDonald, who had fallen whilst in the prison's exercise yard and broke her thigh bone, had been neglected for eighteen days and her injury left untreated; both Con and the victim had begged the authorities for an x-ray examination, but this was rejected. At the expiration of her sentence, Mrs MacDonald was discharged to an outside hospital where an operation was performed, but due to the inferred neglect of her injury, the poor woman was left lame for life. Mrs MacDonald was later awarded £500 compensation for the treatment she had received whilst in the prison hospital, with the help of a committee that had taken up her case.

In the same year that Con experienced her first prison stay, her sister Betty, who was also interested in women's suffrage, joined the Conservative and Unionist Women's Franchise Association (CUWFA), which had been formed the previous year. The association had close links to the moderate National Union of Women's Suffrage Societies, where members were Suffragists as opposed to the more militant Suffragettes of the Women's Social and Political Union. Betty then became president of the Edinburgh branch of the CUWFA shortly after.

While recovering from her prison sentence, Con wrote to Arthur Balfour, her brother-in-law, the former Prime Minister and current party leader for the Conservatives, noting that her brother had discussed with Gladstone the subject of women's suffrage and that he had replied, 'Have women in any numbers asked for it?' Con, as a result, had gathered some published articles with statistics on this subject and passed them on to both Victor and Betty, hoping that they would share this information with Mr Balfour. Unfortunately, they had been unable to do so, and as such she thought the best plan would be to send them to him directly. Balfour had said previously in the House of Commons regarding female franchise:

> Depend upon it this question will rise again – menacing and ripe for solution and it will not be possible for this house to cast it aside as a mere speculation plan advocated by a body of faddists. Then you will have to deal with the problem of woman suffrage and to deal with it in a complete fashion.

In a further letter to Mr Balfour, Con pointed out that the use of the vote was not compulsory and that even further extensions to the men's franchise had been met with opposition by men of all classes themselves. Balfour had suggested to her that the facts were not easy to obtain, and that the opinion of the majority was unattainable in regard to the removal of sexual inequality. Con pointed out that even in 1892, Mr Balfour had made the same remarks even though women's opinion on the same subject was far less established. The Women's Temperance Association was cited by Balfour as inconclusiveness of proof as to the demand for votes for women as this type of association was seen as sprouting propaganda. But also, after an annual meeting in 1893, the new President of the Women's Temperance Association, Lady Henry Somerset, a campaigner for women's rights, had instigated a vote as to whether to make women's suffrage an integral part of the association's campaign, which in turn had caused discord and friction within the organisation and as a result many members had left. In contrast, Con pointed out that if men were disenfranchised at the time of a recent Licensing Bill, if an appeal for their vote had come from an Association of Amalgamated

Brewers, would their interest have been discredited because they needed the vote to improve their personal interests?

On 23 April 1909, Con wrote a note to Annie Kenney from Trewartha, Weston Super Mare, thanking her for 'All the glow and life you put into me from your flowing living self in these few hours we have been together.' Con explained further, 'I was so down, so smashed and failure-filled it was all I could do not to throw up the Bath Plan.' Con also mentioned in her letter that she wanted to ask Annie and Mrs Pethick-Lawrence about tackling women's suffrage in Hertfordshire and that she perhaps might also go to Ireland with her sister Betty to attempt something similar there.

In another letter written on the same day to her Aunt T, Con advised that she had heard from her publisher and that the *No Votes for Women – a reply to recent anti-suffrage publications* pamphlet, was doing really well. Initially Con had tried to publish her suffrage-related writings in an article she had offered to Mr Leo Maxse, the anti-suffrage editor of the *National Review*. However, he had rejected it by saying that 'female suffrage would be worse than a German invasion in the way of national calamity'. Instead, Con had published the work as 3d pamphlet, with Aunt T offering her an advance on the cost of printing and publishing. Con now pointed out she would never have written the pamphlet but for Aunt T's generous financial loan, adding that she was experiencing 'absolutely agonising anguish' over her talk in the village of Knebworth, which she felt was an 'absolute farcical fiasco', but that she had not disgraced herself the previous day at Bath as she was 'buoyed' up by Annie Kenney and Mrs Pethick-Lawrence.

Writing at the end of May from Somerset Terrace, Con referred to her hornet bluebottle job, saying that she was very busy with no time to write letters. She hoped that Sir Edward Grey was satisfied that his government would guarantee the vote next year, but that his guarantees must be publicly manifested and sound.

Betty also wrote to Dolly Gladstone in May saying that, 'My sister Con is going abroad with Mother on 17 June. Do you think it is possible that Mr Herbert Gladstone could meet her, it would bring a lot of pleasure to Con if she could see him but she would understand if he was unable to?' Betty advised that she could bring Con to him, or he could lunch with her at Emily Lutyens' house. However, in June, Robert Cecil penned a note to Mr Gladstone saying that he had heard Con was out of the country, so now any 'personal' interest in the 'Question' (meaning the women's vote) was now abated bar public interest.

In June, Con wrote a strongly worded letter to Mr Arthur Balfour from Homewood. She said she was disappointed as she had heard that there had been a discussion between him and Mr Asquith in regard to a consultation about the suggested Reform Bill, and that a decision had been made that 'nothing in the direction of Women's Franchise needed to be done by either party.' She stated that she thought Mr Balfour had advocated the Votes for Women cause for years and that such a public statement had been made and reported on, and this new decision would therefore be 'injurious' for the cause and also for his position as Conservative party leader. The comments made between the government officials were published in *One New Age* on 3 June and Con consequently enclosed a cutting of the newspaper article with her letter. She was misguided, however, in thinking she could change Balfour's mind, as even his close relations were suffrage supporters and had not been able to sway him.

Later that month, Con, her brother, and her mother travelled to Austria to Villa Anna, in Thumersbach, Zell am See, where she frequently wrote to Victor, fretting about women's franchise. She said that his speech on 15 June at the St James Theatre was well reported in *Votes for Women* and that Mrs Pethick-Lawrence would like to reproduce it as a leaflet. Whilst Con was away, another deputation took place in which Mrs Pankhurst slapped the face of a policeman so that she would be promptly arrested. The action was reported by the newspapers as a 'violent assault', and Maurice Baring promptly wrote to Con declaring, 'I have read much suffragist literature lately. Your pamphlet is admirable. But I am *miserable* at Mrs Pankhurst having slapped the policeman, if it is true. I do think it is a huge mistake, and sends my sympathy bounding off.'

Con instantly wrote a letter, in relation to the Mrs Pankhurst incident, to *The Times*, defending the actions of her friend and stressing why she felt her leader had been compelled to commit this act, because less militant actions were not furthering the vote. To her surprise, the letter was published in full:

WOMAN SUFFRAGE

To the Editor of The Times

Sir, For some weeks past I have been out of England, and have had the disagreeable but enlightening experience of following the English woman suffrage movement, not as for the last nine months it has been my privilege, at first hand, but from the position of the average looker-on. *The Times* is the only English newspaper that I see here daily, a friend sends me occasional cuttings from the *Daily News*, and from these reports and those of the Austrian Press (inspired, of course, from the tone of the leading English journals) I am informed that in a recent 'suffragette disturbance' Mrs Pankhurst, without apparently, any provocation, struck a police inspector in the face; according to *The Times* she 'dealt him two severe blows'; in the *Neue Freie Presse* she 'struck him twice in the face with all her might'; and one article described how the policeman, with the greatest forbearance, did not arrest Mrs Pankhurst until after she had struck the second time. With such information as this, supplied with a colouring of abusive contempt, as the only published evidence available here, it has been difficult to explain to my Austrian friends that the leaders of this movement are not the reckless hooligans that one would suppose from these accounts.

I have had to remind them that these women are driven to struggle for political liberty not merely on the grounds of a theoretic right, for the redress of a merely technical injustice, but because they know that the present political disabilities of women injuriously affect the very root and fibre of national life, of racial existence. No woman of reasonable intelligence could pass a month in Holloway prison and not realise – if she had not realised it before – that that harbour where human wreckage is driven in, is not only a result of human frailty, but also the result of state of law and public opinion from which the representation of the woman's point of view, of the woman's interest, is mainly absent, and which is, therefore, unjust to women and injurious alike to men, women and children. The truth of these facts, the urgent need for their redress, burns in the hearts and minds of these women, to the extinction of their regard for the ordinary political questions of the day as matters of comparative unimportance.

In judging the actions of these women it must be remembered that all available means for bringing forward their cause have been ignored or treated with contempt by a Cabinet of whom three quarters, according to the Chancellor of the Exchequer, are in favour of the demand; and that a large majority of the present House of Commons are pledged supporters of it; also that this manner of presenting their claim, by deputation to the King's Ministers, is absolutely legal. Not even the bitterest enemies of this movement have suggested that it is otherwise; not one of the members of these many deputations, when arrested, has been charged with that as an illegal act. The terms of the charge invariably are: 'for obstructing the police in the execution of their duty,' that duty being to disperse the women who have assembled in this lawful manner to present their just claim. It must from the outside be recognised that to be turned back without achieving their purpose is not amongst the alternatives permissible to the women who fight for this cause, any more than it has been to any other pioneers who have set themselves the task of removing a glaring injustice. Their claim is sufficiently well founded to need no excuse for their persistency, even if it were backed by a far smaller national demand than is the case.

In trying fully to explain the situation, I cannot refrain from mentioning a point never referred to in the Press – namely, that in order to justify these arrests on the part of the authorities, some semblance of a street fight is produced; the women are violently knocked about, wrenched asunder from their coupling of two and two, seized by the neck, thrown onto the ground, and sometimes kicked. After myself witnessing and personally experiencing these tactics, I asked the official mainly responsible what was the reason for them. I received the amazing reply: 'The women at one time were quietly arrested as soon as it became obvious they would not go away, but then they complained that they were arrested for doing nothing, so that now they must expect this treatment – they have brought it on themselves.' This, surely, is a strange form of argument. If the women were rightfully arrested for inconveniencing Ministers and the public, why should any heed be taken of their complaints? If, on the other hand, their contention was just that they were arrested for no illegal act, then how can this injustice be righted by the mere addition of violence to them? There is no question of bad temper or personally initiated brutality on the part of individual members of the police force. To their honour it is acknowledged by all suffragettes that, with rare exceptions, the police carry out these most disagreeable duties in the best way that they can consistently with their orders, and that, after the arrests are accomplished, they are considerate and courteous in their behaviour.

In defence of the police the women are rightly reticent of making known the injuries they receive, but obviously it is impossible for a policeman to achieve throwing women to the ground and to be soft handed over the business. From my own experience in this matter, I can honestly state that the process seemed a deliberate invitation to use in return some form of physical violence, so as to hasten the arrest, which was the certain eventual result, and so put an end to treatment not only physically hurtful to oneself, but degrading and ignominious to the spectators, as well as to those who were under orders to inflict it…

Aunt T had liked Con's letter to *The Times*, but reflecting on the matter after the letter was published, Con wished that she had dealt with the point as to why the women wanted to be arrested. It was not that they wanted to be arrested or imprisoned per se, but that the whole point of their deputations, she explained to Aunt T, was that they wanted to be received by the Prime Minister so that he and his Cabinet would take their case seriously. She reiterated a line from Mrs Pankhurst's speech, saying, 'We press our cause in such a way that the government must either do us justice, or do us violence.'

After Con's trip abroad, she continued to tour the country visiting places such as Birmingham and Liverpool on WSPU errands. During the beginning of August 1909, Con penned a letter to Mr Gladstone after hearing of a report about prison conditions. She said that she disagreed that the cells were healthy or that the prison staff would be difficult to improve, instead declaring that the opposite would be her opinion. Con pointed out she knew no female prisoner who would agree with the verdict given by Gladstone about Holloway prison. In discussion with her sister, she said she would not refer to the Suffragettes unless Gladstone asked of them, and in an interview with him she said she spent a lot of time talking to him about the ventilation of the cells, which she believed were unfit places to keep human beings. One cell she and another Suffragette had used to change their clothes in had smelt badly, and she had assumed it was not used as sleeping quarters, but similar cells like it were. In regard to the staff, Con said that the officers held 'fundamental mistaken views' that were alterations of the traditions and regulations in the way they treated their prisoners. However, several members of the staff were good examples of what would be desirable. In terms of food, Con said that it was suitable but perhaps not fitting for some of the more delicate women who were held prisoner in Holloway.

Writing to Victor at the end of August, Con declared that she felt upset and responsible about the 'poor broken leg owner', Meredith MacDonald (the woman who had fallen in the prison yard), and had a sudden desire to tell Gerald (Balfour, her brother-in-law) all about it. She first showed Gerald the papers detailing the story to see how an impartial outsider would feel about the case and then gave him a brief outline of the situation. Con and the others were worried that the authorities might make insinuations and discredit the person concerned in the eyes of a jury. However, Gerald thought these ideas would be ludicrous. The only way the authorities could discredit the case was if they could prove that the lady in question's previous life affected the condition of her bones. As such, Gerald believed that she would have a very strong case and she should go ahead with the legal proceedings, with the Home Office certainly paying out considerably rather than letting the matter become public. Gerald was amazed that the Home Office overlooked a paragraph in recent communications where a charge of injurious negligence was made against them. He thought that the weakest part of the case would be where a certain Dr English was called in by the prison doctor after the lady in question was released. Dr English's decision not to operate had ruined the chances of good recovery.

When Jessie Kenney, Vera Wentworth and Elsie Howey assaulted Prime Minister Herbert Asquith and the Home Secretary Herbert Gladstone while they were playing golf in early September 1909, the population was shocked. This included the Blathwayt family, who had even built a summer house in their grounds and called it 'The Suffragette's Rest'. The family would invite women to stay there, particularly those that needed to recuperate from prison, and in early 1909, Colonel Linley Blathwayt, a keen horticulturist, had decided to create an arboretum in the field next to their home. Over the next few years, around sixty Suffragettes would plant individual trees to create a plantation that would be known as 'Annie's Arboretum'. Con was one of those with a tree; a conifer planted in her name on 23 April 1909. The Blathwayts disapproved of the Suffragettes' latest militant action against Mr Asquith and Mr Gladstone and refused to condone such methods, with Emily Blaythwayt withdrawing her name from the WSPU membership list. The family even told the Suffragettes that they were no longer welcome at their home, Eagle House, in Somerset. Despite their differences, the plantation remained named after Annie Kenney and continued to be tended by the family, who would frequently post cuttings in their letters to her. Sadly, the plantation was destroyed by property developers in the 1960s and only one tree remains in situ.

In another letter written to Annie from Homewood, Con states 'It's just simply harrowing the Birmingham episode. Mrs Pankhurst and Mrs Lawrence are both ill with it.' The 'Birmingham episode' Con refers to here in her letter relates to a speech Prime Minister Asquith was planning to give in a local hall, which was interrupted by the Suffragettes. One intrepid Suffragette even threw slates from the roof, and five women were arrested in total. Con pointed out to her friend that 'as soon as the public realise it and the "laughter" it has caused in the House(!)...these heroic women will be only too glad, one knows they are only too proud to have been pioneers in this receiving of the Gov'ts new violence.'

Con wrote to Gerald's brother, Arthur Balfour in September 1909 hoping that he would agree to meet Christabel Pankhurst and that he would not find the suggestion impertinent. She insisted that it would be a private interview and the public need not be aware that it had taken place. Con explained that she believed the question of women's franchise was very serious and urgent and that Mr Balfour should give the question much consideration as he has not really had a chance to do so since his speech on the Women's Bill of 1892. She repeated his words back when he had foreseen a time when 'This question will again arise, menacing & ripe for solution.' She stated that this prophecy was now fulfilled and while a further male franchise extension seemed likely, women would once again be excluded. It was her belief that if one important man would champion the cause on their behalf, the women's struggle would soon be at an end.

In mid-October Con wrote to her brother Victor worrying about the injustices and brutalities that were being felt by the suffragists at this time. She said that their mother 'was wonderful' while Con was in prison, and wrote her lovely letters, but that she had not been back five minutes before Con realised her mother was condemning her inwardly while standing by her outwardly. Edith did not want to know Con's physical experiences and was unmoved by hearing about her friends' experiences, which Con said she had only avoided by the snobbery in her case. After receiving no reply from Arthur Balfour, Con once again wrote to his brother Gerald at the beginning of October, reminding him of her request and pointing out that in the event of a general election, the leaders of the WSPU, of which she was a member, would ask to see him in an official and political capacity for an interview. She felt that it would be in both parties' interest that he accepted a private, informal interview, as she had previously suggested/requested, so that he could be up to date on the latest particulars. In a further letter to his latest reply, Con said that there was no question of a 'deputation' and that she would not force a personal interview if he did not want one. Balfour had said to her that he found it 'impossible to approve much that has been going on lately in connection with the suffragist agitation.'

In one of Con's regular letters to Annie Kenney, she mentions how busy she was with WSPU speaking engagements that were booked in Birmingham, Liverpool and other districts during October and November, but that she would be free to speak for Annie on 2, 3 and 4 January and a week on from these dates. She added that 'I improved a little in my speaking with practice in Scotland tho' on occasions I was very bad. I hope to be better & more reliable before I come to you.' Con was pleased to see that there were more politically minded people in Scotland and that they understood the WSPU's fight for women's suffrage more so than people in England.

On 9 October, Emily Wilding Davison and Con were in Newcastle to hear the Chancellor of the Exchequer David Lloyd George speak. Con had travelled there with Jane Brailsford and Christabel Pankhurst and the ladies were to take part in an organised demonstration (using physical violence) against the attitude of the Liberal government towards women. The demonstration was also an attempt to protest against what was seen as the barbaric practice of forcible feeding – particularly in the case of the working woman, Mrs Leigh, who was at the time undergoing this practice in Birmingham prison.

Con wrote about the protest in *Prisons and Prisoners* and how they had attacked the ministerial cars as they drove through Newcastle. Both Emily and Con rushed the car of Sir Walter Runciman, which was driving through the crowd, the two ladies having mistaken it for the one Lloyd George was travelling in, and attempted to throw stones at it. Con's stone managed to hit the car, on the radiator, but Emily did not have an opportunity to throw hers. They were both taken to local police court and Con was charged with assaulting Sir Walter and of damaging his motor car to the amount of £4. She was subsequently sentenced to one month's imprisonment. Emily Davison was released.

According to Christabel Pankhurst's account of the day, Con's stone was labelled: 'To Lloyd George: Rebellion against tyrants is obedience to God.' Con wrote in *Prisons and Prisoners* that her stone throwing 'must be more zealously done, more deliberate in its character than the stone-throwing at ordinary windows...I was determined that when they had me in court my act should inevitably be worse than that of other women.' It would appear that at this time, Con still had an odd balance between her militancy and her urge to not do any harm.

The following night Con wrote an inscription on the wall of her cell: 'TO DEFEND THE OPPRESSED/TO FIGHT FOR THE DEFENCELESS/NOT COUNTING THE COST.'

On 11 October, in the police court, Con's charge was reduced to disorderly conduct and she was given one month in second division or lieu of finding sureties to keep the peace. Between the 11th and 13th, Con carried out a 56-hour hunger strike and on the 13th, her heart was examined by a specialist and she was released from prison. On 22 November, a statement was published by the Home Secretary in relation to Con's treatment:

In view of the repeated statements which the Secretary of State has made in Parliament, he can only regard the statement that Lady Constance Lytton's release had anything to do with her rank or social position as a willful and deliberate misrepresentation. She was released solely because she was suffering from serious heart disease, and because violent resistance on her part to the medical treatment appropriate to her case would have involved some risk to her life.

In October, another Suffragette called Kitty Marion joined forces with Emmeline Pethick-Lawrence, Jane Brailsford and Con to write a letter to *The Times*, emphasising their continued commitment to the cause:

We want to make it known that we shall carry on our protest in the prison cells. We shall put before the government by means of the hunger-strike four alternatives: to release us in a few days; to inflict violence upon our bodies; to add death to the champions of our cause by leaving us to starve; or, and this is the best and only wise alternative, to give women the vote.

Further special activity by the Suffragettes and 'wild recrudescence' of violence were described by the *Northern Daily Telegraph* on 11 October in conjunction with Mr Lloyd George's visit to Newcastle. In the early hours of Saturday morning, the windows of the Liberal Club were smashed with bricks and the following four women were arrested by the police for this offence: Lily Asquith, Violet Bryant, Ellen Pitfield and Dorothy Shellard. The four were brought up before the magistrates and charged £3 7s 6d for the damage, before being sent to prison for fourteen days.

The *Manchester Courier and Lancashire General Advertiser* detailed on 14 October how Con and the other ten Suffragettes who had been arrested at Newcastle had written from the city's Central Police Station requesting that the press grant them their last opportunity to give their thoughts before they endured what awaited them in prison. They also wanted it known what further action they were prepared to take while incarcerated, and how they were going to carry on their protest from within their prison cells. The ladies appealed to the government to give in to their demand and find reasonableness and grant the vote to the 'duly qualified' women and, as such, they would then serve their full sentence obediently and quietly. The ladies added that they appreciated the kindness shown to them by the prison authorities and that no attempt had been made to feed them forcibly, unlike some of their Suffragette friends. In the meantime, both Mrs Brailsford and Con were released the previous evening, despite both having been sentenced to a month's imprisonment.

Con had tried to encourage the young Winifred Jones not to protest at Newcastle, but this was to no avail as Jones was arrested for breaking the windows of the Palace Theatre, her first arrest. Elsie Howey was arrested in sympathy for the cause and called out 'No Surrender' to Constance in her cell. *Votes for Women* described Elsie Howey as 'a devoted Honorary organiser who gives the whole of her services and the whole of her life to the Cause. She is a beautiful, refined and charming girl.' Elsie was arrested several times, including during the window-smashing campaign on a March evening in 1912, and also played the role of Joan of Arc at the funeral of Emily Wilding Davison in June 1913. Elsie Howey passed away in a nursing home in 1963 from chronic pylonic stenosis, a condition which was almost certainly connected to her numerous forcible feedings whilst in prison.

In a letter appealing to the MPs and their constituents, Con wrote to the editor of the *Yorkshire Post and Leeds Intelligencer*. The letter was published on 14 October 1909 with the headline LADY CONSTANCE LYTTON AND HER STONE THROWING:

To the Editor of the *Yorkshire Post*

Sir- As a stone-thrower suffrage cause, I should tell your readers how that women of the most normal type, publicity hating and peace loving, come forth day by day in ever increasing numbers to fill the ranks of the militant section of the suffrage movement. As far as our demands are concerned, we have taken every means to make it clear that we ask for no new franchise laws, nor do we ask that any privileges should be given to women. Certain qualifications have been laid down as carrying with them the right of the Parliamentary vote, and we claim that duly qualified people should vote, whether they be men, or whether they be women. The present basis of the franchise would give the vote to about a million and a quarter women; of these a great bulk would be women, the bread winning class, who support themselves and often their families as well...This charter of liberty is as necessary to women as to men. Every human being who enters the world passes in through the gateway of a woman's body. While women are held in contempt and their interests neglected, the development of humanity is crippled at its birth. We call upon all women who feel for this cause to declare themselves for us. Our violence and our suffering will not always be linked with the symbols of shame. In the days to come, it is not always those who have fought in this good fight, but those who have stood out from it, that will be branded with disgrace – Yours, etc., CONSTANCE Lytton Cell No2, Central Police Station, Newcastle.

Con was seen to challenge Mr Gladstone by ensuring that she was force fed during her 56-hour hunger strike, but instead he was reported in *Votes for Women* to have 'behaved in the way in which bullies invariably behaved,' and that 'while continuing his disgraceful conduct towards working women, he cringed towards those in high places.' Gladstone, apparently, sent a specialist to the Newcastle prison to examine Con. She had waited in her dirty cell, holding her nostrils so as to challenge the act of the forced feeding she was anticipating, expecting the doctor to arrive having at this point gone for so long without food. Instead, the doctor found evidence of serious heart disease and so Con was released as she could not be forcibly fed in her condition. The same treatment was meted out to Jane Brailsford, who as the wife of a well-known Liberal journalist was also regarded as a person of importance. Con felt ashamed when she was released because of the state of her heart. In response, she wrote a letter with Jane Brailsford to *The Times*, pointing out the 'glaring partiality and injustice' that wealthier Suffragettes were benefiting from. Con felt that the main reason she was released was not because of her heart at all, but because of her family connections.

After Con had been released from Newcastle, she made a speech at the Queen's Hall. Edith wrote to Adela saying that:

Our dear Conny got through her speech very well yesterday, and Emmy said the speech made every one weep. She caught the 6.18 train, to my joy, so that I could take care of her, and she was so gentle, and much happier. Oh, the worry of the battling life for her and me! When the misguided ones take to shooting, besides trying to commit suicide, it will be misery and agony, no matter what forcing it brings on any Government, and it will remain wrongdoing that I can't think justifiable.

In November Con was speaking every day, if not twice a day, in cities such as Birmingham, Liverpool and Manchester, and enjoyed meeting different Suffragettes across the country. On the 10th, the *Dundee Evening Telegraph* published a story about Con under the headline 'Why She Became a Militant Suffragette', painting Con as a famous celebrity. The ladies of the Liverpool branch of the Women's Social and Political Union had organised a series of meetings in the city. The first of these was addressed by Con, who said that the reason for her conversion to the cause was that 'it had seemed to her, at one time that it did not matter whether they obtained the vote in three or twenty years, that the longer it was put off the better women would be fitted to exercise it.' Now she thought exactly the opposite. She was impressed with the urgency of the question and believed the sooner they got the franchise the better they would be fitted for it. She declared she was in favour of the militant methods because all lawful and constitutional means had been exhausted without avail.

Con was wary of becoming a representative feminist figure as a result of the special treatment she had received from the authorities. After she was released from one of her prison stints, she learned that she had been accorded certain privileges because her brother, Lord Lytton, had interviewed the head of the Prison Commissioners Department. However, these privileges and conversations could, in turn, disrupt the prison's power over its prisoners by forcing the wardresses to treat her differently, thus reversing the dynamics between Con and her gaolers and perhaps resulting in the punishment of other women: the wardresses.

Whenever Con found herself together with Emmeline Pankhurst, she discovered feelings of pleasure and was 'overcome by the sense of being superfluous'. When the duo visited a newly released hunger striker, Con observed that Pankhurst closely resembled a figure that she had previously ridiculed in a Fra Angelico painting, as Emmeline 'looked ethereal' and had 'a look of purity that no living creature has.' However, Con always felt lowly in such company because of her ongoing physical frailty and for having such a recognisable name, despite the fact that her surname did indeed give her a special power to campaign for the cause.

On 29 September the Home Secretary Herbert Gladstone had informed the House of Commons of his decision to introduce forcible feeding. It was, in his opinion, the only way women's lives, which were sacred, could be preserved, as releasing prisoners in order to prevent them from starving to death was making a mockery of the law. Liberal journalists such as Henry Nevinson and Henry Brailsford argued this decision in a letter to *The Times* newspaper, saying that Gladstone was ignoring an alternative option, which was to recognise the Suffragettes as political prisoners.

Herbert Gladstone wrote to the Fabian Society on 22 November stating that in view of the repeated statements the Secretary of State had made in Parliament, he could only regard the statement that Con's release had anything to do with her rank or social position as wilful and a misrepresentation. He added that 'She was released solely because she was suffering from serious heart disease, and medical treatment appropriate to her case would have involved some risk to her life.'

Con wrote to Mr Balfour in December, noting that his Conservative Party manifesto would be published shortly, and that the WSPU hoped their cause would be alluded to in this publication. In the same month, Kitty Marion, along with Con, received WSPU hunger strike medals 'For Valor', and no doubt Con would have been humbled to have received such an award.

On 16 December, the *Bradford Daily Telegraph* wrote that Con and Adela Pankhurst (the ex-organiser of Bradford) had appeared as chief speakers at a demonstration in favour of Votes for Women at the Mechanics Institute the previous night. It was said that a fair proportion of men had attended this lecture and listened without interruption to the speeches. Con's speech mentioned that only the militant tactics of her sisters (Suffragettes) were mentioned in the press, such as the stone throwing, and other actions were overlooked. Con declared that she was a confirmed suffragist before she went to Holloway, but that 'the faces of the women she saw inside were like many blue books come to life staring her in the face.' Adela Pankhurst reiterated that Mr Asquith's recent statement regarding women's suffrage was not enough in the view of the WSPU, and that he had not promised that if such a motion was introduced, it would not be talked out or shelved. 'If it hadn't been for the Press we should have got the vote long ago,' she declared, 'and if we don't get the vote some women will die under forcible feeding.'

The *Dundee Courier* of 21 December reported that Dundee Suffragettes had attended a meeting at Gilfillan Hall where Con, along with Mrs Flora Drummond and Mrs Mildred Mansel, were the chief speakers. Con was introduced using Lord Curzon's phrase as 'a howling female dervish'. Meanwhile, at the Mathers Hotel, Reverend M. Grant presided over the lecture introducing Con as the granddaughter of Sir Edward Bulwer-Lytton 'one who lives against the immortals in the world of literature.' At this meeting, Con spoke for a full hour, mentioning her chance meeting with Mrs Pankhurst and Miss Annie Kenney, where the question of class 'disabilities', as Con called it, came up. She described how Annie Kenney said that it was not class disabilities that troubled her as much as sex disabilities, and they had both asked her to study this question. Mrs Mansel also spoke and both she and Con urged upon all that were present to help their movement as it would not only benefit women, but the whole world at large if their cause was recognised.

Chapter 5

Becoming Jane Warton, 1910

The Selina Martin incident towards the end of 1909 confirmed Con's suspicions that prisons were treating inmates differently based on class. In this case, Selina Martin, a 27-year-old servant from Lancaster, was allegedly brutally tortured by the prison authorities whilst undertaking her fourth prison sentence for militant activities, this time for throwing a ginger beer bottle through an open window of Prime Minister Asquith's car. Con discussed her thoughts with another WSPU member, Mary Gawthorpe, whilst in Manchester, and Mary confided to her, with tears in her eyes, that most women prisoners were 'quite unknown – nobody knows or cares about them except their own friends. They go to prison again and again to be treated like this, until it kills them!'

A leaflet entitled 'A reply to Mr Gladstone' was issued with the 65th edition of *Votes for Women*, which included the written testimony of Selina Martin as to her experiences of forced feeding. The statement was a response to the government's claim that Selina had been treated as per the rules for untried prisoners, and that no force had been used against her 'beyond what was rendered necessary' regarding her attempts to starve herself and her destructive behaviour:

> We arrived at Walton Prison on Tuesday, the 21st, and the following morning I broke my windows, fourteen in all, and barricaded my cell, and managed to keep the officials out for some time, but eventually the principal wardress got in with others, when they fell on me and beat me unmercifully.

They pulled me off the bed and threw me on the floor. Then the doctor came and told me he would not let me go without food, but would feed me right away. He then ordered me to be dressed in my own wet clothes, and I was taken to a cold, damp cell without ventilation and was handcuffed behind and left on the floor. At night I was taken to a larger cell and kept in irons. Thursday night I was thrown down, then turned over and frog-marched up some steps, letting my head bump up the steps and thrown down. I have had a frightful struggle every time they have come with the instruments of torture, which the doctor does not hesitate to swear about because I ask for a woman doctor. When I complained to the visiting magistrates about the brutal treatment meted out to me, they only replied, 'Well the Wardresses were justified!'

Con had written to say that the WSPU had been 'distressed beyond words to hear of the sufferings of Selina Martin and Leslie Hall.' Her mind was made up. The altogether shamelessly preferential treatment Con had received compared to the others in Newcastle, except for Jane Brailsford, was unacceptable. This event was later referred to by Con in her memoir as the one that had spurred her into taking on a new persona: Jane Warton.

Con had also recently been reading publications about valiant women such as Violet Bryant, who had written a piece for *Votes for Women* saying how during her prison experience, she had told a prison doctor who had examined her heart prior to a series of forced feedings that: 'You have my body, and can do with it what you choose. I can't stop you. My spirit sits serene and smiling above. I can't help crying at times, but it is only because I have not got my body under sufficient control. It is only the body that cries, not the spirit. You can't touch that.' Statements about forced feeding made by other Suffragette prisoners helped others like Con to understand the process before they too underwent the procedure.

The day before Con morphed into Warton, 14 January 1910, she went to stay with her friend Dr Alice Ker. Whether or not Dr Ker was party to Con's plans, no one knows, but Con's mother certainly believed Con had conspired with others to pull off the stunt, even though Con had flatly denied this. Con was desperate to go to prison in disguise and experience the forced feeding, as well as to expose the double standards in British prisons. To do this, she needed to break all the prison rules.

Con thus became determined to see whether the prison authorities would still heed her need 'for exceptional favours' if they did not know who she was. Here began her plan for becoming Jane Warton, a woman who was the complete opposite of Lady Constance Lytton. Con might have gained the idea for Jane from the working-class Suffragettes Annie Kenney and Hannah Mitchell, who in turn donned fashionable clothes and wore furs in order to look upper class and avoid scrutiny from the police. Con wrote in her book *Prisons and Prisoners*, 'I disguised myself by doing my hair in an early Victorian way, so that the police, if on the look-out for me, should not recognise me and so not be tempted to arrest me; for people whose relatives might make a fuss effectively are considered awkward customers.' Con decided that Jane Warton would be a working-class seamstress. She removed the initials from her underwear, cut her hair short and wore a parting not too dissimilar from an early Victorian style. She wore a tweed hat with a bit of tape reading 'Votes for Women' interlaced into the hat band, a woolen scarf and gloves, pince-nez glasses, and finally pinned small, china brooches of Mrs Pankhurst, Christabel Pankhurst and Mrs Pethick-Lawrence to the collar of a long green coat, which only cost her 8s and 6d. Her costume was complete. The name Jane may have been chosen because Joan of Arc was the patron saint of the Suffragettes and Warton was similar to Warburton, the name of a sympathetic supporter of hers. There was also a degree of iconography within the Suffragettes, with heroines such as Emily Wilding Davison, who was later crushed by a horse at the Derby in 1913, and Con's martyrdom as Jane Warton furthering the imagery of the New Woman; those who broke the old ideas of how a woman should behave. These independent women who stood up to voice their opinions on social subjects became role models for the next generation.

Con was not just a person of solemnity and martyrdom. She had inherited her father's love of amateur theatricals and frequently fell into fits of giggles. To modern eyes, the surviving photograph of Con in her Jane Warton outfit looks almost like she is playing the part of a transvestite, with shades of Dame Edna thrown in. Gathering all the parts of her planned ensemble took careful thought. She visited separate shops in Manchester to pick up each individual item so as not to raise suspicions and visited a 'frowsy little hairdresser's shop' to have her hair cut in a short and unbecoming style, with 'smooth bands down the side'.

On 14 January 'Jane' attended a protest meeting against forcible feeding outside Walton prison. The meeting was initially addressed by Mrs Sarah Jane 'Jennie' Baines, a full-time organiser for the WSPU. Con spoke up from the crowd, begging people to go with her to the governor's house but was subsequently arrested for exhorting a crowd to protest, as well as for dropping stones over the prison governor's hedge. After Con was arrested, her disguise must have been ridiculous as her fellow prisoners tittered in the waiting rooms. It was all she could do not to laugh at herself. On 15 January she was sentenced to a fortnight in the third division and hard labour, with the option of a fine. Two days later she was put into a punishment cell for refusing to perform hard labour sewing exercises. The punishment for this was a bread and water diet for three days, but

Right: Con as a child (left) with her sister Betty (right) and their mother Edith, taken in India in the late 1870s. (*Knebworth House Archive*)

Below left: A picture of a teenage Con taken in the early 1880s. (*Knebworth House Archive*)

Below right: Con appearing frail after several illnesses, circa 1899. (*Knebworth House Archive*)

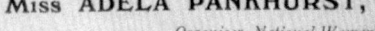

Above left: *Votes for Women* postcard of Adela Pankhurst, circa 1908. (*Women's Library*)

Above right: *Votes for Women* postcard of Annie Kenney, circa 1908. (*Women's Library*)

Left: *Votes for Women* postcard of Christabel Pankhurst, circa 1908. (*Women's Library*)

Above left: *Votes for Women* postcard of Mrs Pankhurst, circa 1908. (*Women's Library*)

Above right: *Votes for Women* postcard of Mrs Pethick-Lawrence, circa 1908. (*Women's Library*)

Right: Con pictured in 1908. (*Prisons and Prisoners*)

Above left: Lord Victor Lytton, Con's brother. (*Knebworth House Archive*)

Above right: WSPU photographic portrait postcard, 1910. (*Women's Library*)

Left: Con as Jane Warton pictured in 1910 near Liverpool's Walton prison. (*Prisons and Prisoners*)

(Left to right) Annie Kenney, Con and Emmeline Pethick-Lawrence at the Suffragette arboretum, 1910. (*Women's Library*)

Walton prison, Liverpool, where Con/Jane was held. (*Prisons and Prisoners*)

Above left: Con seated for portraits, 1911. (*Women's Library*)

Above right: Lady Constance Lytton proudly wearing her medals, 1912. (*Women's Library*)

Left: Con with fur, date unknown. (*Knebworth House Archive*)

Above and below: Two photographs of Homewood taken by Mrs Jenkins, the housekeeper, in 1923. (*Knebworth House Archive*)

The mausoleum where Con's ashes are interred. (*Knebworth House Archive*)

instead she decided to refuse both. In her memoir, Con wrote that during her nights of hunger, she dreamed of 'fruits, melons, peaches and nectarines, [the] end of a moonlit balcony that was hung with the sweetest smelling flowers.'

On 18 January she was fed by force at 5 pm. Before the first instance of forcible feeding, neither her pulse was taken nor her heart checked. After a struggle, the doctor inserted a steel gag which fastened her jaws wide apart, opening her mouth far wider than normal and causing intense pain. Con described the procedure as follows:

> He put down my throat a tube which seemed to me much too wide and was something like four foot in length. The irritation of the tube was excessive. I choked the moment it touched my throat until it had got down. Then the food was poured in quickly; it made me sick a few seconds after it was down, and the action of the sickness made my body and legs double up, but the wardresses instantly pressed back my head and the doctor lent on my knees. The horror of it was more than I can describe. I was sick over the doctor and wardresses, and it seemed a long time before they took the tube out. As the doctor left me, he gave me a slap on the cheek, not violently, but as it were, to express his contemptuous disapproval.

She was returned to the ordinary cell that night.

On 19 January, as a point of protest, Con broke the glass from a gas box (gas lamp) inside her cell. She was taken before the governor for this, but he deferred the punishment for the judgement of the magistrates. On her third forced feeding experience, Con started to shiver uncontrollably, but still no one took her pulse or checked her heart. She had been slapped by the doctor leading the forced feeding and told that if she vomited again, she would be force fed again.

Con felt great pity for 'Jane', as she felt that it was 'as if I were outside of her'. She attempted to protest to the prison governor at the harshness of her treatment, despite how abnormal looking she was with her short hair. On 21 January, Con was brought before the visiting magistrate, who deferred their judgement and adjourned the case, with appointment date for resumption.

Con's heart had been given a cursory examination by a junior doctor, who she claimed listened to a mere two beats, before pronouncing it to be 'splendid'. The short examination was negligent, but Con had decided to withhold the information that she had valvular heart disease. It was public knowledge that Con had issues with her heart, but as Jane Warton, such information was kept private. All militant Suffragettes who went on hunger strike put their health and lives at risk, regardless of any underlying health conditions, but it was even more dangerous for Con, especially after a doctor had previously advised that she risked paralysis or even death if she went on hunger strike. Con had been examined by a Dr Marion Gilchrist, the first woman to receive a medical degree in Scotland. The report had noted that Con had 'a chronic valvular lesion' but it was 'acting well in spite of the fact that she had just undergone great exertion.' This condition should have been easily picked up by a doctor.

This forced feeding experience was repeated another seven times before it was discovered that Jane Warton was really Con in disguise, and she was therefore immediately released on 23 January, having been forcibly fed since 18 January. Con had been losing weight at the rate of 2 pounds a day and was pronounced to have been released on medical grounds. However, shortly after her initial arrest, the Press Association had contacted Con's family, from whom she had kept her intentions a secret, for confirmation that she was imprisoned once again in Liverpool. Con wrote in her book *Prisons and Prisoners* that a Prison Commissioner at the Home Office had confirmed there was a prisoner in Walton prison 'whom they for some days suspected of being other than her declaration'. After her release, Con's sister, Emily Lutyens, was told by a Dr Price that he had never seen such 'a bad case of forcible feeding' and that she had been 'practically asphyxiated every time'.

Meanwhile, Prime Minister Asquith had called a General Election in early 1910, which was held between 15 January and 10 February. He had declared that he would not resume his office until he was given the powers to overthrow the veto of the House of Lords. When he was reminded of his promise to introduce the Reform Bill during the Parliament that was as such brought to a premature end, he made the following affirmation that may have made him look better in the eyes of the Liberal women:

> Nearly two years ago I declared on behalf of the present Government that in the event of our bringing in a Reform Bill, we should make the insertion of a women's suffrage amendment an open question for the House of Commons to decide...Our friends and fellow workers of the Women's Liberal Federation have asked me to say that my declaration survives the expiring Parliament, and will hold good in its successor, and that their cause, so far as the Government is concerned, shall be no worse off in the new Parliament than it would have been in the old. I have no hesitation in acceding to that request... the Government...has no disposition of desire to burke this question. If clearly on which a new House of Commons ought to be given the opportunity to express its views.

The WSPU branded the statement as worthless, and although militant action was suspended during the election, their previous militant 'soldiers' were still being forcibly fed in the Liverpool prison. Con was still devoted in her loyalty to those at Clements Inn and was desperate to act in solidarity with those hunger strikers. She visited

Mary Gawthorpe, who had been incapacitated by a long illness, and it was her words that helped Con make up her mind, despite fearing that her plan of action might be 'displeasing to her leaders', as she later recalled.

Christabel Pankhurst wrote to the playwright George Bernard Shaw, a fellow Hertfordshire resident and member of the Fabian Society, enclosing a description of Con's recent experience in prison. Christabel explained that Con had proved Mr Gladstone to be guilty of immense cruelty, untruthfulness and snobbery, adding that when he ordered Con's release from Newcastle prison, it was only because of her social position. This was already evident for all to see, but now he had had 'Jane Warton' forcibly fed there could be no doubt about the matter. Christabel hoped that an end would be put to the way Suffragette prisoners were treated, as well as an end to forcible feeding.

Below is the full description of Con's experience that was sent to Bernard Shaw:

PRISON EXPERIENCES OF JANE WARTON (LADY CONSTANCE LYTTON)

After a hunger-strike of nearly 4 days (89 hours) I was fed by force without my heart being tested or my pulse felt. I was fed twice a day through the mouth by means of the stomach tube (the mouth being forced and kept open by a gag) until my release on Sunday morning, January 23rd. The operation invariably induced vomiting. In spite of the first hand accounts I had heard of this process, the reality surpassed all that I had anticipated – it was a living nightmare of pain, horror and revolting degradation. The sensation is of being strangled, suffocated by the thrust down of the large rubber tube which arouses great irritation in the throat and nausea in the stomach. The anguish and effort of retching while the tube is forcibly pressed back into the stomach and the natural writhings of the body restrained defy description. There is also a feeling of complete helplessness, as of an animal in a trap, when the operators come into one's cell and set to work. I think while I live I shall not forget the sensation with which I watched the changes of light and listened to the sounds that foretold the return of the visitors to my cell.

Except in the way of clenching my teeth I offered no resistance, and after the fourth or fifth time I succumbed to the pain of being forced by the steel gag and opened my jaws with a very brief protest. After the first time the doctor as he left me gave me a slap on the cheek, not violently, but apparently to express his contemptuous disapproval. I said to him the next day – 'Unless you consider it a part of your duty, would you please not strike me when you have finished your odious job'. He gave no answer but never repeated the probably half-unconscious insult. The second time the vomiting was more excessive than the first – a most revolting and exasperating business of the doctor and attendants as well as for the prisoner. And no adequate precautions were ever taken for these invariable consequences. The doctor was angry and left my cell hastily saying, 'you did that on purpose: if you do it again tomorrow I shall feed you twice.'

The next day I remonstrated with him explaining that I was a small eater and that the capacity of my body was very limited, that if only he would give less quantities the result might be better. I also begged that he would not press the tube so far down into my body. He treated these suggestions with contempt saying that anyhow my stomach must be longer than his since I was taller than he was. He, however, granted my request to sit up in a chair instead of lying flat on my back.

This third time I vomited continuously but in spite of this the tube was not removed and the doctor continued forcing in more food. The result seemed to surprise and to slightly alarm him, and he called in his assistant to test my heart; after a brief and very superficial investigation it was pronounced quite sound and the pulse steady. I myself told the doctor that I was not liable to faintings or collapse. I did not mention the slight chronic debility of which the Home Secretary had made so much and which, of course, would have disclosed itself under any thorough investigation. In Newcastle a specialist had been called in and my heart tested with elaborate paraphernalia for ten to fifteen minutes; but now the same heart belonged only to Jane Warton. From that time, however, the doctor's manner became more considerate and even kind, and I noticed a change in the way I was treated generally, so much so that I imagined my identity had been discovered. It seems, however, the Authorities had only begun to suspect I was 'somebody else'. A fellow suffragist, Miss Brown, who suffered from like but much worse symptoms than mine, was kept in Holloway and forcibly fed through the whole term of her imprisonment of four weeks; she is still in a nursing home where the severe gastritis induced by this 'life-saving' process will probably require treatment for at least two months.

The morning after I had first been fed by force, I protested by breaking the thick glass of the 'gas box' between my cell in the passage. I expected, of course, to be put in hand-cuffs for this as others had been for breakage of much less valuable window glass. The Governor, however, deferred my punishment to the judgement of the visiting magistrate who again deferred the matter <u>sine die</u>. It will be interesting to see what steps are eventually taken against Jane Warton for this offence, a graver one than that for which two women are now serving several weeks of imprisonment although they had already suffered prison punishment at the time.

A later newspaper report published after Con's death stated that following her release, she was so terribly emaciated that for months afterwards she could not sit in a chair to take her meals but had to kneel on a cushion instead. Additionally, two of her teeth had been injured by the gag and as such her mouth was so painful that she had to have dental treatment.

When writing to her sister Betty Balfour on 24 January, Emily Lutyens explained how she had learned about Con's situation in full:

> I want to write to you a full account of what was described on the posters yesterday as 'Lady Constance Lytton's latest Freak.' You know that we have been worried at getting no news, and on Friday afternoon I telephoned to Christabel, who assured me she was all right [sic] and electioneering at Southport...On Saturday morning I read in *Votes for Women* of the Liverpool arrests, and felt sure Con was the Miss Warton referred to. Saturday night I was dining with Mrs Webb when, about 8.30, a telephone message came through from Ned at Knebworth to say they had received a telegram from the editor of the *Weekly Despatch*, saying they believed Con was in prison under an assumed name. I immediately telephoned Mr Chapman and begged him to try and get official information. I won't tell you how he managed, as I promised not, but about 10.30 he turned up at Eaton Square, having found out that Jane Warton was to be released, as [she] was steadily losing weight. The authorities were delighted to be told who she was, and that someone would go and fetch her. We telephoned the prison doctor at Liverpool, and he said he would expect me at 7 a.m. Sunday. I got home

at 11.20, woke up Nannie to explain matters, hastily got 'some rags and a bug,' and caught the 12 o'clock train to Liverpool. I slept, and had a kind lady in my carriage, who told me how to reach my destination on arrival. We got in at 6.30. I took a Hansom up to Walton gaol. Thick snow everywhere, and Liverpool like a city of the dead. Not a soul astir but street sweepers. Not a light in any house.

I arrived at 7.30 at the doctor's house, and he rushed out to welcome me…He was very obsequious to me, I was in my best dress from the day before, which made a very good impression. He offered me tea, and then we sat down to talk. He told me that neither he nor his colleagues had found anything wrong with Con's heart, but he had never known such a bad case to feed, as it seemed always to asphyxiate her. That she had steadily lost weight, two lbs a day he said, and he could not keep her, as he could not nourish her by feeding. He told me that his suspicion had first been aroused by the ill-concealed delight of one of the other suffragettes at hearing Warton was being fed. Then on Saturday morning she consented to taking a meal of bread and milk as she felt she was failing, and she wished to go through with her sentence. This immediately showed him she was different from the others. Then he told me of his description of her to the Home Office, which gave me fearful giggles, which I could hardly restrain. 'I said she was 5 ft. 9 inches, that she was spare, that she should weigh 148 lbs., and only weighed 110. When it came to the nose I did not exactly say it was large, but that it was somewhat Wellingtonian.' This [was] all told [to] me in a melodramatic voice.

At 8.30 we started for the prison and were shown to the Governor's office. I thought him rather a kind man with a military manner. He and the Dr. went off to tell Con she was free and I had come for her. The Governor returned in about 10 minutes to say she was very happy and would be able to travel, that they must give her a meal, and she would be almost an hour. He kindly took me into his house for breakfast, and he and his wife were very kind. Evidently the wife had no sympathy with the prisoners in general, and said she never saw them. At about 10 I was fetched back to the Governor's office, and there by the fire stood a figure in a green serge coat, somewhat prison like in character, and with quite short curly hair, like a dark Fraülein Oser. This was Con. She had a little argument with the doctor, and then I took her off. She is terribly thin, her face so drawn and pinched, but a good colour, and I think very pretty with her short hair. Her body just like the pictures of famine people in India. I took her off to the hotel, and she had a hot bath and a good breakfast, which she greedily ate, and we started home by the 12.50 train. She talked without ceasing all the way up.

After Con was released and was recovering at 29 Bloomsbury Square, her sister Emily's house in London, she wrote to Mrs Mansel describing her joy at being home:

What a wonderful letter from you. Thank you, my darling. It was all a nightmare, nothing else, and yet mine so much less long than all the others forcibly fed have endured. I can't cover nor warm my bones, and feel flimsy and brain light. Otherwise well, and oh! The joy that I really do believe I have done some good. I speak at the Queen's Hall on Monday, Liverpool following Friday. After that I am only to lie fallow for long. It is sad that my darling Mummy only feels disgraced and injured.

Once, when staying at Emily's house, a Miss Brackenbury (probably either Marie or Georgina, who were both British painters and Suffragettes) visited Con while she was resting and quite immobile because of illness. Miss Brackenbury asked Con's little nephews, 'Are you not proud of your splendid auntie?' To which they answered, 'No, we think she has done very wrong!', again reinforcing the opinions of the Lytton family regarding Con's actions.

After her release, and despite feeling desperately weak, Con tried to write and lecture as much as possible about the conditions she and other Suffragettes endured whilst imprisoned. On 28 January, *Votes for Women* printed a response to Con's account, 'In view of the important statement by Lady Constance Lytton which appears in this issue, our readers are invited to make every effort to increase the circulation and bring it to the attention of our friends.' On the same date, the *Torquay Times and South Devon Advertiser* wrote that 'In October of last year the Home Secretary stated in the House of Commons that I [Con] was released from Newcastle prison, after 2 ½ days hunger strike and without being subjected to forcible feeding, solely because I suffered from serious heart disease.' The Home Secretary had said that her suggestion she had been released because of her rank or social position was a willful and deliberate misrepresentation.

On 31 January, the Queen's Hall had been packed for a reception to show appreciation for Con's splendid actions in Liverpool. It was reported in *Votes for Women* that her fine speech during the meeting proved how deeply she understood all that underlies the women's movement, and that the speech affected the audience deeply. On 10 February, the Home Office issued an official denial of the truth of the below statements, which had been listed by her brother Victor:

1. That Constance (Jane) was forcibly fed with any previous medical examination.

2. That this forcible feeding was carried out 8 times despite the fact that the prisoner's heart was being damaged in the process.
3. That the method used to force feed the prisoner was carried out in such a way that it would not be allowed in a hospital.
4. That the doctor slapped Constance's (Jane's) face in an angry and insulting way.

There had been a delay publishing this denial as efforts were made to produce a public inquiry of an impartial nature, but this was refused and instead a secret inquiry was carried out. The prison officials also denied the last three statements were true. In Newcastle, Con's heart was examined by a specialist and was told that it was seriously diseased, whereas in Liverpool, a cursory examination of the heart led to the declaration that it was quite sound. When she came to collect her sister, the doctor at Liverpool prison told Emily that Con had been 'practically asphyxiated every time that she was fed by force'. It was rumoured that the officials had come to believe her statements were based on hallucinations she had experienced through hunger striking, but those who knew her personally believed that they were true.

In February, a Parliamentary Committee led by Con's brother Victor, the Conservative Earl of Lytton, and Henry Brailsford, attempted to bring together pro-suffrage MPs, regardless of their party background, to draft together a women's suffrage bill based on collective agreement. Brailsford's wife Jane was a militant Suffragette, but Brailsford himself had been trying for some time to persuade the Liberal government to take action on women's suffrage. Together the two men persuaded the Pankhursts to declare a temporary truce and set about drafting a women's suffrage bill. It was to be named the Conciliation Bill and was seen across the country as the best hope for women since the 1884 Reform Act. Victor became chair of the committee, and the WSPU paused their militant actions with the hope that they had already done enough to convince the government of the necessity for action and change.

Victor supported his sister not just at home, but through the Conciliation Bill, as well as drawing public attention to his sister's prison ordeals. Con hoped that his position within the House of Lords would help publicise the lives of all women, not just those of the leisured classes, and that they too would 'burst through the gilded bars which hold their own lives in bondage' to relieve their own imprisonment. In *Prisons and Prisoners* Con asked, 'And why are these women imprisoned? Because they and many thousands, or rather several millions, of women with them, have asked for the vote, but the government would not give it to them.'

Prime Minister Asquith received a deputation from all societies. Annie Kenney, a member of the Militant Party, believed that they were admitted on sufferance, as it were, because they were the only people the Prime Minister feared. She wrote, 'I was present, though not as a speaker. Lady Constance Lytton and I were together. Mrs Asquith stood behind us all the time.'

The first draft of the bill was to give female property owners the vote, but no other women. In cases where a man might already be named as the property owner at an address, the woman could not claim to represent that property. Although the bill would hardly be a radical proposition, the suffrage community would still see it as a triumph. The Conciliation Bill would later be introduced on 14 June under the ten-minute rule and pleasingly won by a majority, which was required in order to secure time for a second reading. Asquith announced that this would be on 11 and 12 July. If the Conciliation Bill had become law at this time, Con could have, quite rightly, claimed that she had played a major role in helping British women receive the vote.

On 4 February, *Votes for Women* had quoted from the *Liverpool Courier* reporting on Con's imprisonment:

> Mr Gladstone's declaration that under his administration, no distraction based on class difference should be allowed in the treatment of Suffragette prisoners, has been put by Lady Constance Lytton to a test which doubtless never entered into the Home Secretary's reckoning. She has proved Liberalism is of the familiar type that respects, not persons, but personages, especially titles...Mr Gladstone was indignant when he found that this tender concern of his for her ladyship's physical weakness was twisted by the unscrupulous Suffragettes into an expression of deference for a title; and he implied that under his *regime* a weak heart would exempt any imprisoned Suffragettes from the feeding tube.

The official line offered by the prison authorities was that their staff treated all prisoners the same, regardless of their backgrounds. However, members of the WSPU begged to disagree and became very suspicious, including Con, who was to all intents and purposes an upper-class spinster, who felt that she had been treated differently whilst an inmate at Newcastle prison. Despite going on hunger strike like the others, she had not been forcibly fed and was released after only two days, the official reason given because of her heart. Con believed that it was more likely her brother, the Earl of Lytton, had political connections as he was a member of the House of Lords and that this had influenced the prison authorities.

Although Con's actions had proved to herself, and later to others, that there was a genuine difference in the treatment of women from different backgrounds, sadly the conditions and actions she endured had taken a great toll on her health and she never recovered from the short time she had spent as Jane Warton.

After Con was released, the harsh treatment meted out to her was revealed to the press and became a national scandal. Indeed, it would seem Victor was somewhat moved by her bravery and wrote both a letter to *The Times* newspaper and to his friend Winston Churchill, who was now the Home Secretary. Writing on 18 March Victor said that 'I quite understand that with all you have to attend to in taking over a new office...but I was getting rather unhappy at being so long delayed from publicly vindicating my sister against the charge of untruthfulness which was brought against her by the Home Course.' He added that 'The fact that my sister concealed her identity & refused to answer medical questions does not relieve the prison officials at Liverpool of any responsibility. The fact that they knew nothing of her physical condition made it all the more incumbent upon them to find it out for themselves.' Victor also pointed out that Con had been resting for two months after being released from Walton prison, had received careful medical attention and treatment for her heart condition, and yet was still in a bad way. He concluded his letter by saying he had 'never asked for special consideration for my sister. I only pointed out that Jane Warton had not received that careful medical examination which your predecessor publicly declared was the indispensable preliminary to forcible feeding in the case of every prisoner.'

There was controversy between Edward Troup from the Home Office and Victor Lytton as to the accuracy of Con's statements and the huge difference in treatment between herself and 'Jane Warton'. As Jane, Con had refused to answer any medical questions, but neither Con nor Jane had refused a medical examination from the prison doctor. At this juncture, Herbert Gladstone retired from the Home Secretaryship and Winston Churchill became the 'prison secretary' in his place.

Victor said that the differing treatment of the 'two' women was a case of double standards. He called for a public inquiry to ensure that all women who were imprisoned were treated fairly. Sadly, the inquiry never happened, but a short time later, in March 1910, Winston Churchill did introduce Rule 243A, where Suffragettes could enjoy a slightly more lenient stint in prison as long as they had not been sentenced for any type of violent crime. The rule stated that prisoners who were of the second or third division could enjoy some first-division privileges such as receiving letters from home, being able to read books and being able to wear their own clothes. Forced feeding had ceased, temporarily. The new rule detailed:

> In the case of any offender of the second or third division where previous character is good, and who has been convicted of, or committed to prison for, an offence not involving dishonesty, cruelty, indecency, or serious violence, the Prison Commissioners may allow some amelioration of the condition prescribed in the foregoing rules as the Secretary of State may approve in respect of prison clothing, bathing, hair-cutting, cleaning of cells, employment, exercise, books and otherwise. Provided that no such amelioration shall be greater than that granted under the Rules of Offenders of the First Division.

The benefits of Rule 243A could be withdrawn in the event of misconduct, but the fact the government needed to introduce this measure was seen as a small victory for the Suffragettes.

Prior to the rule being introduced, one prison governor had experienced Suffragettes who had told him, 'with the most refreshing candour that, unless they were treated as first division prisoners and political offenders, they would break every prison rule in existence and take no food'. In February 1909, both Con and Mrs Pethick-Lawrence had told the governor of Holloway prison that they would not cause any trouble as long as their demands were met. Defiance of this kind was common place from the Suffragettes, and the Home Office was concerned that imprisonment would become meaningless due to the stress of trying to maintain prison discipline, while being met with wide-scale defiance from the competing demands of these prisoners.

Politicians were accused of disregarding any medical investigations into forced feeding and its damaging effects. In 1912 Charles Mansell-Moullin, a surgeon and lecturer, would collaborate with the dermatologist Agnes Savill and the renowned surgeon Victor Horsley to put together an extensive report into forced feeding that was published in the *Lancet*. Their report was damning, suggesting that forced feeding caused both physical and emotional effects on the nervous system, including neurasthenia (mechanical weakness of the nerves). Other prisoners could suffer mental anguish and psychological trauma at hearing the cries, choking and struggles of their comrades. The authors accused the Home Secretary of regularly deceiving the public by claiming that 'artificial feeding' was indeed safe and that he had been assuming the reports sent by prison doctors had played down the physical and mental experiences of those who had endured forced feeding.

Con had alleged that working-class Suffragettes were imprisoned and force fed for much longer periods than their peers as they had less social influence. These women were less likely to publicise their experiences and the State, which knew that forced feeding was possibly illegal and potentially immoral, was less likely to inflict the practice on those who had 'a louder social voice'. Forced feeding had been used for a while in asylums on the mentally ill, but it had been decided by the authorities that the Suffragettes had defective minds as they were deliberately disobeying prison regulations. The prisons were hopeful that the Suffragettes would be deterred from their actions by being force fed, but instead the opposite happened; their spirit and resolve would not be broken.

Con asked the prison doctors, who believed that they truly were saving lives by performing these medical procedures, why did they not extend the same treatment to all patients regardless of their class or notoriety? Another suggestion is that the prison doctors were simply unsympathetic to these rebellious prisoners, whose bad behaviour disrupted the normal day-to-day life of prison medical practices, and, as such, meant they received harsher punishment from doctors, who were much more willing to inflict abuse and pain.

Ethel Smyth wrote in *Female Pipings in Eden* that, 'Hunger striking was becoming rather the rule than the exception...It was three years since Marion Wallace-Dunlop, the first hunger striker, had shown the way, two years since Lady Constance Lytton as "Jane Warton, seamstress" and two others had been forcibly fed.' She added:

> ...after thoroughly overhauling his prisoner, the prison doctor declared that Lady Constance Lytton's heart was far too weak to allow forcible feeding. Whereupon she was released – of course without signing any sort of undertaking to abstain from militancy. About a fortnight later, strange to say, this very same heart, as tested in the body of one 'Jane Warton', an obscure militant of the working class, was pronounced to be perfectly sound; so 'Jane Warton' was forcibly fed. And when Constance Lytton had more or less recovered from this hideous experience – curtailed probably by the inevitable leaking out of 'Jane Warton's' identity – in her very first public speech she called attention to the many obscure suffragettes tortured and broken by forcible feeding as she was, from whom an indifferent world would withhold even such grudging recognition of their heroism as is bestowed on the high-born lady in disguise.

Forced feeding was described by Herbert Gladstone, the Home Secretary, as 'special treatment for self-starvation' during questions in the House. It was also justified as a prevention of hunger-strikers from committing 'the felony of suicide', as cited by Henry Bull Templar Strangways, a former Australian politician, in *Votes for Women*, published on 8 October 1909.

'The experience in prison this time was intensely grim and dreadful, but now the reward seems undeservedly great,' Con wrote to her fellow Suffragette friend Alice Ker from her sister's flat in London. She added, 'To think that I who have suffered by far the least of all the "forcibly fed" should be making people wake up more than all of them.'

Three years later, in 1913, the Home Office would come to believe that the WSPU was encouraging those 'abnormal and neurotic' people who were likely to take part in militant behavior. These militants were being chosen to commit punishable crimes, and were seen as 'weaklings' who had physical defects and would cause much embarrassment to the government. One confidential report at the time had determined that of the recently imprisoned female population, the majority had more underlying health issues than the average member of the general public. These included people suffering from seizures, those with mental health problems, those who had recently suffered a nervous breakdown and people who were 'eccentric'.

After Con exposed the prisons for their differential treatment, the *Liverpool Courier* reported that 'Lady Constance Lytton seems to me to have caught out the prison system, if she has caught out nothing else…This does not show that the authorities were wrong in their treatment of Lady Constance Lytton. It does show that they were seriously wrong in their treatment of the working class.' Christabel Pankhurst saw it as a signal victory over the government.

Emmeline Pankhurst, the founder of the WSPU, was personally horrified by the screams of fellow women being forcibly fed during her stay in Holloway, writing afterwards that:

Holloway became a place of horror and torment. Sickening scenes of violence took place almost every hour of the day, as the doctors went from cell to cell performing their hideous office…I shall never while I live forget the suffering

I experienced during the days when those cries were ringing in my ears.

On one occasion when the prison officials tried to enter Emmeline Pankhurst's cell, they found her standing there with a clay jug raised above her head declaring, 'If any of you dares so much as take one step inside this cell, I shall defend myself'.

In April 1910 Con wrote to Edward Marsh, Winston Churchill's private secretary, enclosing an article she had written that had been published in a recent edition of *Votes for Women* so that he would know her views. She had heard a rumor that Wilfred Blunt, the political essay writer and poet, had wanted her to meet both Churchill and Marsh, and said she would love to meet them to discuss prison reform and how successful the borstal system was. Con was always hopeful that, through her family connections, she could sway politicians into putting through the vote.

After turning down a request to give a speech, Con sent a letter to Annie Kenney on 12 April writing 'It is dreadful to refuse you, especially as I believe to be alongside you would do me an immense amount of good just now. But my body is still on strike.' She added that, 'I am concentrating my power on the Glasgow exhibition – I am booked to open it on the second day, April 28th.' Despite both her doctor and her 'people' not recommending she appear, she felt she should do so regardless and would base her decision as to whether she could accept further engagements on how she felt afterwards. She concluded the letter with, 'I have been struggling for a week with an article for *Votes [for Women]*. My brain simply won't work & the vain effort makes me fearfully deprest [depressed]. I daren't undertake real meeting speeches while like this.'

In May Con wrote to her brother worrying about the burden that the Woman Suffrage Parliamentary Committee might have on him, asking if he might want to place it onto someone else's shoulders.

Although she did not want him to think she believed he was not doing a good job, or that others could do it better, she was simply concerned about the added pressures it put on him. This was particularly true as King Edward VII had died that month and so the country probably had other concerns at the time.

In June, the WSPU put Con on the payroll as an organiser, so as to counteract the costs of her tours, where she spoke about her experiences and the comparison of her incarcerations in prison both as Con and as 'Jane'. She was paid £2 per week, which was enough for her to rent a small flat, just off the Euston Road, meaning she was now able to spend Monday to Friday away from the restrictions of living at Homewood with Edith. She felt 'highly honoured' and 'on her modest stipend', although living sparsely, she was happy to be still working for the cause. She wrote to Aunt T:

> Have I yet told you? I am now to be a paid organiser of our Union! They have been most generous, and paid me backwards for the last six months. The pay is £2 a week and all expenses connected with the work. It will mean the week days away from home but every Friday to Monday free. Wondrous terms; in return I give all I have to give, night and day, year in and year out. Mother on the whole pleased, and feels it to be flattering.

That month, Dr Mary Gordon, the first British female prison inspector, visited Con and her mother. Edith liked Dr Gordon and was able to have a lengthy discussion with her about Con's situation and, in turn, Dr Gordon told Edith about the great public service Victor had done with the Conciliation Bill and how it was recognised. Con wrote to Victor and told him how pleased all the 'leaders' such as Mrs Pethick-Lawrence, Christabel, and Mary Gawthorpe were with his work. She added that a small contingent of ten or eleven women would go from Knebworth to the 'walk', a five-week pilgrimage culminating in a Hyde Park address to over 50,000 people. Con had never seen Clements Inn anywhere like it. Later that month she read in the newspapers that the Nationals (The National Union of Women's Suffrage Societies, led by Mrs Millicent Fawcett and company) had suggested that they were satisfied in regard to the second reading of the bill. Con feared that if nothing could be done, however, then militancy may have to restart and she hoped to be able to carry out her duty, just as her brother had done on the Conciliation Bill itself.

On 12 June Con wrote to her sister-in-law Pamela, declaring she was overjoyed at having read a government report of a Ruggles-Brise talk. Sir Evelyn Ruggles-Brise was chairman of the Prison Commission and wanted to combine reform with deterrence and to separate young criminals from older men in prisons through the Gladstone Committee. On another note, she hoped that one day Pamela would no longer be upset and worried about seeing Victor's name as one of the foremost in Con's cause. She pointed out that despite more boys being born than girls, the boys were more delicate and died during infancy because of the conditions their mothers lived in and that the strain of motherhood could be quite tremendous.

On 18 June there was a meeting at the Albert Hall and a 6-mile-long procession that took three hours to pass by. Con was just about well enough to walk in the procession, along with her sisters and Neville. Lord Lytton was the chief speaker at the meeting, and Annie Kenney later wrote that 'We all liked him...[he] had shown a genuine desire to get the problem which absorbed us really settled. The truce was still on, but we were sowing good seed and reaping in so many ways rich harvests.' A total of £5,000 was raised on the day, with the money helping to pay for the manufacturing and selling of Suffragette merchandise, travel costs, and the printing of *Votes for Women*.

'*The March of the Women*', a song composed by Ethel Smyth in 1910 to words by Cicely Hamilton, was dedicated to the WSPU and became the organisation's official anthem, replacing 'The Women's

Marseillaise'. It would certainly have been in Con's mind during this new period of her life and was no doubt sung at the various meetings and processions that took place during the year and in the years to come. The tune was adapted from a traditional Italian melody, with the following lyrics:

> Shout, shout, up with your song
> Cry with the wind, for the dawn is breaking;
> March, march, swing you along,
> Wide blows our banner, and hope is waking.
> Song with its story, dreams with their glory
> Lo! They call, and glad is their word!
> Loud and louder it swells,
> Thunder of freedom, the voice of the Lord!
>
> Long, long, we in the past
> Covered in dread from the light of heaven,
> Strong, strong, stand we at last,
> Fearless in faith and with sight now given.
> Strength with its beauty, Life with its duty,
> (Hear the voice, oh hear and obey!)
> These, these – beckon us on!
> Open your eyes to the blaze of day!
>
> Comrades – ye who have dared
> First in the battle to strive and sorrow!
> Scorned, spurned – nought have ye cared,
> Raising your eyes to a wider morrow,
> Ways that are weary, days that are dreary,
> Toil and pain by faith ye have borne;
> Hail, hail – victors ye stand,
> Wearing the wreath that the brave have worn!

Life, strife – those two are one!
Nought can ye win but by faith and daring.
On, on – that ye have done
But, for the work of today preparing.
Firm in reliance, laugh a defiance,
(Laugh in hope, for sure is the end)
March, march – many as one,
Shoulder to shoulder and friend to friend.

Although the Conciliation Bill would pass its second reading with a majority of 109 votes, Prime Minister Asquith decided against passing it, instead preferring a new bill that would give universal suffrage to men. Following the failure of the act, Betty Balfour, Con's sister, spoke at the Conservative and Unionist Women's Franchise Association's (CUWFA) platforms across the country, including places such as Kendal, Ulster, Gloucester and Penzance. She had privileged access to Members of Parliament, making her popular with women's suffrage members, and politicians respected her views. The *Bath Chronicle* ran a feature regarding the dresses worn by the CUFWA attendees, with Betty reported on one occasion to have been wearing a black velvet dress with delicate lace at her throat and wrists, matched with a black toque. Her speaking commitments to the cause at this time stayed heavy, and although she frowned upon the violent tactics used by the Suffragettes, Betty remained on good terms with her sister and her comrades in the WSPU, but did raise the funds to reconstruct a Medieval church that was burned down by the Suffragettes in East Lothian.

Chapter 6

Declining Health and Stroke, 1910-1914

It was reported in the *Bristol Times & Mirror* on 24 January 1910 that:

> After serving nearly a week's imprisonment at Walton gaol under an assumed name, Lady Constance Lytton was released yesterday morning, and handed over to the care of her sister. Lady Lytton's identity remained unknown at the gaol until Saturday...when released yesterday morning she was in a very weak condition...the local suffragettes say it is a wonder she was not killed by the treatment.

The writer Marie Mulvey-Roberts suggests that it was precisely because of her family connections that Con was able to inspire the suffrage movement to which she belonged, as she provided women 'with such a powerful role model of moral courage'. The American historian of women's studies, Martha Vicinus, quoting from Mrs Coombe Tennant JP's letter of condolence after Con had passed away, also believed that 'the idealism of the WSPU found its highest expression in Lady Constance, whose pilgrimage highlighted the path for countless others, yet was also representative of "the spiritual history of unnumbered women of our class, which led to the breaking of shackles".'

When Con was the chief speaker at the WSPU meeting at the Queen's Hall, Westminster, in January 1910, she pointed out that not every prisoner had had their heart examined, and that her disguise was easier than she thought it would be. When some items of hers had been taken from her at the police station, she noticed that there was a handkerchief of hers that she had forgotten to remove her name from. Worried that the handkerchief would betray her, as a precaution she threw it into a fire and the authorities ignored her actions – she later said that they were so used to Suffragettes doing strange and unusual things that they took no notice. She said that on this occasion when she began her hunger strike, whilst posing as Jane Warton, there was no medical examination. When it came to force feeding her, the doctor did not even feel her pulse but set to work at once to force feed her while the wardresses held her in place. She explained that the pain of the forced feeding was so great that she forgot everything, including the cause, other women and to her sorrow remembered only her own sufferings. She said that a gag was used and her mouth was forced wide open. She thought that this was quite unnecessary and explained to the doctor that he might try a different method, but her suggestion was treated with absolute contempt and she felt that as a Suffragette, she was not worth listening to at all. She described her prison experiences as a living nightmare but reminded her audience that a total of thirty-five women had been force fed so far and 'of these women I have suffered the least'. Con always preferred to downplay her experiences in prison, wanting her listeners to be horrified at what had happened to the Suffragettes as a collective, not the injustices committed against a lady such as herself.

It was reported in the *Daily Gazette for Middlesbrough* on 10 February that:

The Home Secretary has addressed a letter to a correspondent who called his attention to a leaflet which has been circulated recently with reference to the imprisonment of Lady Constance

Lytton; the suffragist, at Liverpool. He says:- 'The statement that Lady Constance Lytton was released from Liverpool Prison only when her identity was discovered was untrue. The release of "Jane Warton" was recommended by the medical officer and authorised by the Secretary of State upon purely medical grounds.' The suggestion that any difference in her treatment at the two prisons, Newcastle and Liverpool, was due to considerations of social position is entirely without foundation and there is no justification whatever for the charges made by Lady Lytton against the officers employed at Liverpool Prison.

The *Manchester Courier and Lancashire General Advertiser* of 17 February then published this short notice: 'Lady Constance Lytton is obliged to cancel all engagements, as she is confined to bed and is forbidden by her doctors to write or receive any correspondence.'

The next day, 18 February, the following was published in *Votes for Women*:

A reply. Lady Constance Lytton's friends desire to say, in reference to this official statement, that the Home Secretary has refused to grant a full and impartial review, at which it was hoped that she would have the opportunity of proving her charge against the officials of Walton gaol, and steps are being taken to request him to reconsider his decision.

A few months later, in the issue of 3 June, *Votes for Women* described how, when it was known that Mrs Leigh was undergoing forced feeding at Birmingham prison, Mr Gladstone was said to have denied 'all imputation of being a "respecter of persons", saying that a weak heart was the sole cause of her release.' But in truth his veracity was to be put under a more severe test than he was expecting, as a few months later stories were being spread about Liverpool prison in regard to Selina Martin and Leslie Hall, women who were both said to have been brutally treated by the prison authorities (see previous chapter).

In an edition of *The Times* from July 1910, Victor Lytton further detailed his sister's two prison experiences, the first under her own name and then as 'Jane Warton'. He declared that he regretted her name should have been introduced into the Home Office vote discussion, although Con was too ill at the time to even hear of the matter. One of the charges that Lord Lytton made against the prison officials on his sister's behalf was that the excessive quantity of food forcibly fed to Con was a wanton act of cruelty and caused acute sickness, yet the process continued. Sir Edward Troup had denied positively and emphatically that the vomiting had taken place, however McKenna had admitted that Jane Warton was released because she was unable to keep her food down. Lord Lytton said that 'when the administrators of the law are driven in their turn to disregard the elements of truth, the very foundations of good government appear to be crumbling away.' Betty Balfour also wrote to *The Times* in support of her sister and spoke of her disgust that the authorities seemed to be suffering from petty vindictiveness and appeared to be compelled to let out the prisoners one by one when they had been reduced to death's door – a course both tyrannical and weak.

Whilst Con was recovering from her prison exploits, she was still trying to establish herself as a writer. A cafe review she wrote appeared on 7 July 1910 in the *Common Cause*. 'Edinboro – Cafe Vegetaria, 3 Nicolson Street. Next door to university. Excellent service from happy and well-paid helpers. The ideal of what such a place should be. Perfect furnishings, food really good, staff intelligent and sympathetic (lowest wages paid, 15s a week of 54 hours, and all meals and uniforms provided),' thus highlighting that Con felt a good employer should appreciate their workers by paying them a reasonable wage.

The *Bath Chronicle and Weekly Gazette* of 29 September discussed a speech made by Con in the city. Con pointed out that Bath was a special place as Annie Kenney was the organiser for the WSPU there, and Annie was a leading light to her in the whole movement; if it was not for Annie, Con would never have joined. 'Her ladyship explained how it was she had come into the front rank of the '"hooligans", to be a stone thrower and gaol bird three times over.' After an initial meeting with Mrs Pankhurst and Annie Kenney, Con had studied the matter of gender inequality for three months and became convinced of the urgency of the situation. She felt that the treatment meted out to female demonstrators was unconstitutional, unjust and unfair. How would men like to be treated? Con did not take on the violent methods until she saw a woman who had come out of prison after having been forcefully fed. She felt angered at this unmedical, inhuman and unhygienic method, so monstrous and barbaric. She too wanted to endure these same trials so that she could understand what these women went through. At the conclusion of the meeting, Mrs Mansel appealed for donations towards the rent of the Suffrage Shop and Colonel Linley Blathwayt was the first to subscribe, giving a sum of £5.

Once again, Con was touring the meeting halls as a speaker. Con and Adela Pankhurst spoke at a suffrage meeting in Sheffield in October 1910 and Miss Pankhurst stated that their union was ready to fight the government, even if it meant that in doing so, they had to sacrifice their lives.

After suffering more significant health issues towards the end of the year, Con was forced to miss 'Black Friday' on 18 November, when Suffragettes storming the Houses of Parliament were beaten and sexually assaulted by the rough handling of the police. Con was now an active worker in the Suffrage Movement, but she had several seizures after speaking at engagements.

On 15 November, the *London Daily News* reported that, 'The absence of Lady Constance Lytton from recent engagements of the suffragists is explained by the announcement that she has been seriously ill with heart trouble. Last evening it was stated at the residence Dowager Countess Lytton that Lady Constance was recovering.'

However, despite being quite unwell, Con appeared in the news again the following year, with the *Cork Examiner* of 15 March 1911 publishing a letter from her, written in London, after Con's name had unexpectedly appeared in *The Times*. Lady Selborne, a Conservative supporter of women's suffrage, had written to the newspaper enclosing a letter supposedly written by Con. Three days later, Lady Selborne wrote again to *The Times* saying that she had forged the letter:

Tuesday Night – The Press Association has received the following letter from Lady Constance Lytton. 'Though I did not actually pen the letter which Lady Selborne sent the press over my name last week...she wrote with my full approbation and I accept complete responsibility for it. In my view one of the justifications for the militant methods is the exclusion by the press of any adequate reports of the constitutional propaganda. Of course it is not, nor the only nor the chief justification which lies far deeper in the right of women who are denied citizenship to rebel against the Government which attempts to coerce them into submission – (signed Lytton).'

Arthur Balfour wrote to Betty towards the end of April, saying that he was unsure as to why his suffrage friends were displeased with him. He pointed out that he had always been a supporter of the movement and did not feel that his opinions had changed at all over the years when the issue had been put both before the country and the House.

He thought that if the subject really was desired by women, then in his judgement the request should be acceded. He was willing to make an appointment to meet with Betty and her Con to discuss the matter further.

Betty sent word to Con that Mr Balfour was willing to see her at 1 pm the following day, 4 May. Con wanted to 'put before him some facts' about the Votes for Women demand. Both Con and Betty wrote a short letter to him explaining that Annie Kenney would be unexpectedly in London on the same day, and would he object if she came along too? Con explained that Annie would speak for the most part instead of Con and would not prolong the interview. She pointed out that he had already met Annie some years ago in Manchester and was impressed with his honesty and straightforwardness. When they met, Annie gave Balfour a flower wrapped in paper. He wrote of this in a letter to Betty saying that he was 'deeply and even painfully moved'. Balfour was in a difficult situation: if he met Annie Kenney, she might take the meeting as confirmation that the vote was closer to a resolution. Although Balfour was sympathetic to the cause, in reality he could not see a way to push the vote through.

In mid-May, Balfour received a worried note from Betty about a letter she had received from Christabel Pankhurst, which she thought he should see. The letter described how Sir Edward Grey and Prime Minister Asquith were to solely decide whether facilitates for the Bill were to be given or not. Sir Edward was to have said the previous year, 'It has been my personal opinion that next year [1911] if the House remains of the same mind, facilities ought to be found for the proper discussion & further progress of the Bill.' In recent conversation, Grey was rumoured to have asked what terms the Suffragettes would agree to. It was a glimmer of hope for the suffrage societies.

Shortly after Con and Annie's visit to see Arthur Balfour, there seemed to be some hope for the Suffragettes, and a possible guarantee that their Bill would be passed in the next parliamentary session. Con wrote again to Balfour, suggesting that if there was a motion for adjournment, could he propose that if there was time for the Scottish Lands Bill, the time could instead be allotted for the Conciliation Bill, pointing out that this request would not be stretching his genuine opinion and that the WSPU would be very grateful.

On 30 May, Con sent the following letter via *Votes for Women* to Arthur Balfour:

THE FAVOUR OF PUBLICATION AS REQUESTED

FACILITIES FOR THE WOMEN SUFFRAGE BILL

The statement made by Mr. Lloyd George on behalf of the government has in no way shaken the belief entertained by the members of the Women's Social and Political Union that the Woman Suffrage Bill can, and ought to be, carried into law in the present Session. If the government can give facilities for another private members measure, the Scottish Land Bill, (and such it is stated is their intention) this in itself is a sufficient refutation of Mr Lloyd George's argument that the government proposals for legislation will so fully occupy the Session that time cannot be found for the Woman Suffrage Bill.

While declining to give facilities for this Bill this Session, the government make what at first sight seems to be a pledge of full facilities next Session, but on clearer inspection it appears to be in reality, not a pledge for next Session at all, but for the third or some subsequent Session. For Mr Lloyd George, though he announced that the government will provide a week for the discussion of the Bill in Committee next Session, gave it to be understood that any further time which may be required for passing the final stages of the Bill will not be provided next Session but in some later Session.

The W.S.P.U. cannot possibly accept such a pledge as this, because, as Mr Asquith has already emphatically stated, under the Parliament Bill, measures which do not pass the Commons in the First or Second Sessions, will not become law in the existing Parliament, but will have to stand over until after the General Election.

Con explained to Balfour that the above letter was written in answer to the government's announcement of the Conciliation Bill. The Committee had suggested delaying it for a week, giving them enough time for the further stages of the process. However, the government had now maintained that a week was insufficient. Unfortunately, the guarantee of acceptance was not assured, and the WSPU needed more reassurance. Con begged Mr Balfour to speak up for the Suffragettes and asked him for a more convincing promise that the Bill would go through.

Con was still very much involved with the WSPU, despite her failing health, and took part in meetings such as the one reported by the *Bedfordshire Times and Independent*, where speeches were made by the Hon. Mrs Haverfield and Con. Admission to the event, in late November, was by ticket and it was said that there was a large and sympathetic audience. The platform and surrounds were decorated with the colours of the union; green, white and violet, and there were large banners proclaiming: 'Deeds not Words', 'The Women's Guise is the Men's', and 'Taxation without Representation is Tyranny'. The paper reported that Mrs Haverfield and Con were members of a deputation which had visited the Prime Minister earlier in the day and that 'It was evident in the ring of speeches that Mr Asquith with assurances had scarcely satisfied the militant branch movement, that the Vote may finally be passed.

On 21 November Con was arrested for a third time, having been found guilty of window smashing, which was part of a mass campaign in Westminster and Victoria. Con enjoyed the experience as she was surrounded by her Suffragette sisters and said that the police were of good humor and even encouraged the Suffragettes in their campaign. Con spent only a few days in prison and there was no forced feeding this time. She was released thanks to an anonymous donor paying for her bail, and a superintendent drove her back to her flat on Euston Road. She had found a few changes at Holloway prison since her previous incarceration there: you could now wear your own clothes and meet and talk in the exercise ground. Soon after, she had a more serious heart seizure which left her paralyzed and bed bound.

Another Suffragette alongside her, Leslie Lawless, was given a much longer sentence. The *Daily Telegraph & Courier (London)* printed a report on 25 November saying that:

> Slow progress was made at Bow Street Police Court yesterday in dealing with the women arrested during the disturbances arising out of the Suffragist demonstration of Tuesday. Two of the defendants were committed for trial, twenty-two sentenced and two discharged. Some 130 cases, more than half of the original number, have still to be disposed of and Mr Marsham will again sit specially on Monday and Tuesday. Public interest in the proceedings had greatly diminished...Lady Constance Lytton and Leslie Lawless were charged with causing willful damage. Lady Constance Lytton looked and was said to be ill, but she declined an offer of an adjournment. Police evidence was given that the defendants broke some windows at the post office in Victoria Street with hammers, doing damage to

the extent of £315. Lady Constance Lytton said this was the only form of protest left to women by a government which refused them the elements of representation. The Magistrate: 'Were you one of the deputations that saw the Prime Minister the other day?' Lady Constance Lytton: 'Yes and I heard Mr Asquith say the Government would do nothing whatever ever for women.' Mr Marsham remarked that from what he saw in the newspapers he gathered that the question was still open. Lady Constance Lytton: 'Yes, it is still open, and while women are alive it will never be closed. Mr Asquith is exactly where he was three years ago, and all our peaceful agitation is absolutely valueless in his eyes.' Mr Marsham: 'I cannot hear political speeches.' Miss Lawless: 'If the fight for one's liberty is a crime, then I am guilty.' Defendants were each fined 40s and £1 17s 6d damage, or fourteen days.

Sadly, Con's heart attacks were becoming more frequent and as she was pretty much confined to her bed, she decided to pen her book, *Prisons and Prisoners*, in order to further expose the influence of class in the treatment of Suffragette prisoners. Some critics at the time saw the book as propaganda material that aimed to startle its readers out of complacency, and to rally them to a widespread injustice that was women's inability to be able to vote. On the other hand, some readers gained a sense that prison held a curious and compelling attraction to Con and offered a powerful alternative to the cloistered life she had been leading, believing it was thrilling for her to experience 'the other side' and be fully immersive in the cause; especially as she was now reaching middle age and was still a spinster. Con feared becoming one of those women whose 'fearful unnecessity of their disablement awakens no pity...a yoke so submitted to, so uselessly endured, can claim no reverence of martyrdom.' However, it was her frailty and her 'disablement' that made her a figure of such high stature and high moral energy as a Suffragette.

When she compiled *Prisons and Prisoners*, which was completed in 1913, she described her experiences as a Suffragette and prisoner. The book was published in March 1914 and reprinted in April and May that year. These personal memoirs present a fascinating narrative of the spirit of sisterhood between the Suffragettes and describe how she was almost penniless, despite being the daughter of an earl, and that she was dependent upon her mother. Her handwritten copy is held in the archives of the Museum of London and her annotated manuscript shows her publishing plans: 'I am aiming at a book of about 300 pages, the cost 2/6d. Sylvia's description of prison gates opening to a prisoner on outer cover. Portrait of me as Con. Another as Jane Warton on the frontispiece.'

The suffragette newspaper *Votes for Women* wrote a glowing review of *Prisons and Prisoners* following its publication in 1914:

All who have the cause at heart must read this splendid personal record of Lady Constance Lytton's imprisonments. Her whole-hearted sacrifices are well known, and this book is the outcome of her observation, reasoning, and dispassionate criticisms upon the prison system of England as applied to women. The acute sufferings that she endured are graphically described. A book of heroism.

In a lengthy review, Mrs Pethick-Lawrence stated, 'Its direct and immediate appeal extends far beyond the confines of any weeniest, however significant and great.' It was the first testimony of a Suffragette to be published in a book, a great deal of the text being based on extensive notes that Con had taken after being held in prison in Liverpool.

In her chapter 'Militancy, Masochism or Martyrdom? The Public and Private Prisons of Constance Lytton', Marie Mulvey Roberts wrote of *Prisons and Prisoners* that 'few more compelling or celebrated accounts of suffragette imprisonment, hunger striking and force-feeding are found.' One of Con's favourite friends, Olive Schreiner, said of it that 'You feel her spiritual beauty all through the book'.

As we have already seen, Con was forcibly fed, even though she suffered from a heart condition. Con was one of a number of militant Suffragettes who included visionary experiences in their writing that aligned themselves with some kind of higher power in antipathy to mortal forces. One such visionary moment from her incarceration in Liverpool's Walton prison was recounted by Con, when she described how the setting sun had created an image of the three crosses of Calvary, a depiction of the crucifixion of Jesus in the open air, and was thought to represent the suffering she had endured whilst being forcibly fed. She also portrayed the current government in her writing as those who had witnessed but would not cease the forced feeding, which was a representative of Christ's crucifixion.

> It looked different from any of the pictures I had seen. The Cross of Christ, the cross of the repentant thief, and the cross of the sinner who had not represented – that cross looked blacker than the others, and behind it was an immense crowd. The light from the other two crosses seemed to shine on this one, and the Christ was crucified that He might undo all the harm that was done. I saw amongst the crowd that poor little doctor and the Governor, and all that helped to torture these women in prison, but they were nothing compared to the men in the cabinet that wielded their force over them. There were the upholders of vice, and the men who supported the thousand injustices to women, some knowingly, and some unconscious of the harm and cruelty entailed. Then the room grew dark and I fell asleep.

Prisons and Prisoners includes a third-person account of Con's shopping trip to purchase the items required for Jane Warton's disguise. In her memoir, Con refers to Jane as a 'Punch version' of a Suffragette. The British weekly satirical magazine *Punch* regularly published heavily stereotypical, comical and negative cartoons about the Suffragette activists. Her disguise was not only a success in that it fooled the authorities, but it also allowed the triumph of turning her into an object of disparagement, with abuse being hurled at working-class Jane, who in reality was the upper-class Constance.

A quick perusal of any descriptions of the forced feeding suffered by many Suffragettes all come to the same conclusions: that the experience was both a physical and mental violation which caused pain, anguish, rage, humiliation, emotional distress and suffering. For some the experience had been likened to rape and methods used varied between prison doctors. But it was also a point of identification and union between many of the Suffragettes, as opposed to an isolated bodily experience. Of particular note is that no matter how much she resisted and suffered abuse from figures of authority, Con never judged the doctors, prison wardresses, police officers or even the chaplain in her book or letters. Instead, she blamed the government for classing the Suffragettes as common prisoners and not as political ones, which she felt herself and her comrades deserved.

One of the last times Con was with her fellow Suffragettes was at the start of 1912, when, dressed in the purple, white and green colours of the Suffragettes, Con, Christabel Pankhurst and the Pethick-Lawrences attended the wedding of the suffragette Una Dugdale and her partner Victor Diederichs Duval at the Chapel Royal, in London. Both were prominent in the suffragist movement. The marriage made the headlines because Una wished to revise the wedding vows and not 'obey' her husband, as part of a demonstration of the emancipation of women. However, she was told on the day that if she did not agree to 'obey', then the marriage would not be legal and so she conceded, although many claimed not to hear her say it during the service itself. Many Suffragettes, as well as the general public, turned up to watch the unique ceremony. Mrs Pankhurst was unable to make her first public appearance after her return from America as her vessel was delayed by quarantine. The bride wore a white satin-rich gown veiled with Brussels' net and beautifully embroidered with a scroll crystal design. She had a court train suspended from her shoulders with silver cords. Her bouquet was of orange blossoms tied with white heather as a tribute to her Scottish associations.

Although Con had faded into the background due to her ill health, her fellow Suffragettes continued campaigning for the female vote, but with a new strategy of sabotage and violence. Con wrote to Mrs Pankhurst on her friend Miss Avery's behalf on 19 February 1912, saying that although Miss Avery would consider it the very highest privilege in assisting the cause on 4 March, she would not be able to because, as a school teacher, 'her imprisonment would mean the sacrifice of her economic independence and would throw her onto her family for support'. This was because the police were now arresting more Suffragettes for their actions.

The deputation invitation that was sent out by Mrs Pankhurst for members to take part in the March 1912 protests read:

MEN AND WOMEN I INVITE YOU TO COME TO PARLIAMENT SQUARE ON MONDAY, MARCH 4TH 1912 at 8 o'clock to take part in a GREAT PROTEST MEETING against the government's refusal to include women in their Reform Bill. SPEECHES will be delivered by well-known Suffragettes, who want to enlist your sympathy and help in the great battle they are fighting for human liberty.

This great militant protest was a skillfully planned secret attack that would involve many women armed with hammers, stones and clubs, and would involve simultaneously smashing the windows of both shops and offices in the West End of London. Letters of reply that were seized in later raids on the WSPU headquarters show the many pressures ordinary women faced and deliberated over when getting involved in militancy, such as the struggle between family pressures and commitment to the cause.

At the appointed hour on the day of the event, women removed hammers from their handbags and took to attacking the shop fronts. The stones and hammers used bore phrases and slogans relating to women's suffrage. Over 100 women were sent to trial following this incident, and for many it was their first offence. The sentences at the trial ranged from fourteen days to six months, with seventy-six women given sentences of hard labour. It was said that the working-class Suffragettes tended to be given the harsher sentences – something that was noted by both the accused and their supporters. Much to Con's disappointment, she had been unable to attend the protest due to her on-going health issues.

As mentioned in *Letters of Constance Lytton*, Con's last letter to be written with her right hand was to her sister Betty, and was written on 3 May 1912, shortly after she had suffered a stroke that paralysed her right side. The contents of the letter still blamed the government's reluctance to grant women the vote and as such, why the Suffragettes still needed to carry on with their militant action.

> As regards the Suffrage prisoners, the whole treatment of them from the beginning is one long thread of tangled misgovernment. Given free play to the ventilation of their grievance instead of sitting on the safety valve, there would have been natural channels through which the pressure of their demand could have acted: petitions read and responded to, deputations received, questions answered at public meetings. Press would have followed with open doors, the thing would

have been instantly recognised as the irrepressible force it is, and M.P.s and Governments would have given way. Once start suppressing a growing vital thing, and you will have to increase your means of suppression whenever the last methods fail.

However, her last letter written with her right hand might actually have been written a day later, on 4 May, to her friend Alice Ker. Whatever the case, Con had another stroke on 5 May, which was believed to have been brought on by the effects of her experiences in prison as Jane Warton. Unfortunately, it proved to be the harbinger of another type of imprisonment. The stroke had followed a series of heart tremors and declining strength. On this occasion she was found by her visiting cleaning woman, collapsed and semi-conscious on the floor of her Euston Road flat. The stroke paralysed her right arm, crippled her right leg and foot and for some time left her incapable of movement or speech: 'I had a stroke and my right arm was paralysed, also slightly, my right foot and leg.' Despite this, she added, 'I am with them [the Suffragettes] still with my whole soul.'

Letters from Constance Lytton describes what happened after Con was found: 'Her sister, Emily Lutyens, was summoned, and she was moved to her sister's house at 29, Bloomsbury Square. She lay there for some weeks between life and death, and finally crawled back to a crippled and invalid existence.'

On 24 May, *Votes for Women* published the following statement regarding Con's condition: 'We have been asked to announce that, owing to ill health Lady C.L. is unable, for the present, to attend to correspondence or make engagements. We are sure that, in expressing our deep regret at her illness and our warmest hopes for her speedy recovery, we shall be fully representing the feelings of all readers.' Olive Schreiner wrote in a letter to a friend a week later that she feared Con was dying because of her heart.

Declining Health and Stroke, 1910-1914

After the effects of her stroke had abated a little, Con was left permanently paralysed down her right-hand side. There was no doubt now that she would ever be able to return to her militant lifestyle of smashing windows or undergoing further hunger strikes: she was to retire to the countryside and leave the Suffragette crusade just as it entered the height of its militant phase. Her fluent letter writing also ceased as she could now only write with her left hand. A nurse, Sister Kate Oram (who had previously nursed Florence Nightingale), entered Con's life on 7 May and would be her companion for six years. Due to her disability, Con's visits were now restricted to her sister Emily, Aunt T and Mrs Pethick-Lawrence.

Gertrude Colmore, who wrote the novel *Suffragette Sally*, debated in her work the issues facing both women and the government, such as those printed in the newspapers and communicated in speeches from speaker platforms on how the right to vote was far more significant than merely the marking of a ballot paper. Colmore also followed through the examination of class issues inside the suffrage movement with her depiction of Con as one of her main characters, Lady Geraldine Hill. Like Con, Lady Hill goes to similar lengths to bring discriminatory class-based prison methods to light. Lady Hill expresses her beliefs in prison reform much the same as Con did, and is also arrested for throwing a stone at a government minister's car. The character was also released from prison for having a weak heart and therefore being too ill for forced feeding. Lady Hill even disguises herself as a working woman, Anne Heeley, who is imprisoned for militant suffrage actions, and force fed after her weak heart is declared sound. After her release Lady Hill uses her social standing to help publicise her discriminatory prison experiences, but fails to convince the government of the reality of what she believed had occurred. Another 1911 novel, *No Surrender*, written by Constance Maud, also includes a character based on Con, this time called Mary O'Neil.

Olive Schreiner wrote to her friend Betty Molteno on 31 May 1912 about what had happened to Con:

> My beloved friend Con Lytton is also, they fear, dying from her heart. A clot formed of the worn out tissue of that dear brave loving heart has got into her brain & she is quite paralyzed. If it moves she may yet live for some time: but I do not wish it if she is to suffer as Ettie has suffered: Oh it's not death one rebels against – one accepts that – but its these awful years of agony before the end.

Con returned to Homewood after her stroke and would spend the next eleven years as an invalid being cared for by her mother. She soon found that the role of an invalid daughter was to be more confining than the restrictions placed on her by her body. Her new disabilities were to prove that it would be even more difficult to earn a living independently. It was terribly ironic that the activism she loved so much had indirectly led to invalidism. She had deliberately endangered her own life when she entered Walton prison as Jane Warton and would eventually trigger the end of her life when she moved away from Homewood in 1923, as we shall soon see.

However, during the first two years after her stroke, Con successfully taught herself, with a patient struggle, to write with her left hand. Her old writing had been fluid and easy, but now her new handwriting was painfully straight, with each letter formed and printed individually. She struggled on in this way until her friends bought her a typewriter in 1917, but among her personal papers, however, there are more handwritten documents than typed, as it cannot have been easy to use the keys with her paralysed hand.

Her first typed letter was sent to Adela Smith on 19 January 1917 and describes her excitement about her new present:

> Adela, A typewriter! The Corona, of the very latest ideal kind, has arrived. Everyone seemed to know it is for me, so I try to believe it. Now I hear you had a big share in giving it to me. How shall I thank you for this wonderful present! It will make the whole difference to my slow writing powers. It is like a fairy gift in a dream and I wake to find it true.

Despite her ill health, Con continued to follow her fellow Suffragette's activities from a distance. She often sent money to those who were in trouble and in 1913, she sent flowers to Kitty Marion, another fellow Suffragette, who was imprisoned along with Clara Giveen for setting fire to a racetrack at Hurst Park Grandstand, in protest after the death of Emily Wilding Davison at the Epsom Derby. Kitty Marion was forcibly fed a total of 232 times during her time as a Suffragette, and Con felt a love for her that she said she, 'cannot put on paper'.

By now, Con was in her mid-forties and, rather unusually for an upper-class lady, was unmarried and childless. However, she explained that her deep interest in prison reform acted as an emotional substitute for 'what maternity there lurks in me'. Her love for the women she met in prison is somewhat evident in *Prisons and Prisoners,* as the 'Dedication to Prisoners', which is given at the front of this book, shows. After her death, Winifred Coombe Tenant, one of the first women appointed as an official visitor to improve treatment of prisons, wrote that Con 'was denied an active life in the tussle of things but her thoughts lived and were worked out by others. She had a share in altering the world and shaping thoughts among them.' Con's book was used as an authoritative text that lower-class women used within their own portrayals of prison. For instance, Olive Schreiner dedicated *Woman and Labour* (1911) to Con:

> Not because I think it worthy of her, nor yet because of the splendid part she has played in the struggle of the women

fighting today in England for certain forms of freedom [but] because she...embodied for me the highest ideal of human nature, in which intellectual power and strength of will are combined with an infinite tenderness and a wide human sympathy.

Olive dedicated Tennyson's poem, 'Wages' to Con because she saw her as woman who had struggled through everything that had been thrown at her to fight for her cause.

> Glory of warrior, glory of orator, glory of song,
> Paid with a voice flying by to be lost on an endless sea-
> Glory of virtue, to fight, to struggle, to right the wrong-
> Nay, but she aim'd not at glory, no lover of glory she;
> Give her the glory of going on, and still to be.

Prisons and Prisoners also illustrates how the prison system was a means of reinforcing gender roles. Con describes in her memoirs how women's activities in prisons focus on cleaning and sewing, which was further reinforced during one of her prison stays when she was given two books. The first was a devotional text and the second, as she termed it, an instructive book on domestic hygiene named *A Perfect Home and How to Keep It*. There was an emphasis on rehabilitating women as good domestic subjects during the peak of the women's suffrage movement.

When the story of her experiences was published, Con asked that the medallion Sylvia Pankhurst had designed for the WSPU might be printed centrally onto the cover. Con originally wanted it to be white because it signified purity, as described in Lisa Tickner's *The Spectacle of Women: Imagery of the Suffrage Campaign (1907-1914)*. During the women's suffrage demonstrations, ex-prisoners would pointedly wear white clothes. However, her publisher, William

Heinemann, contacted Con's brother Victor about the impracticality of having a white colour and so she chose purple instead. For the Suffragettes, purple symbolised dignity, loyalty or courage. Con insisted that any small sums she received in royalties were sent to the *Women's Dreadnought* newspaper. Despite living on small means, Con was a regular subscriber until her death in 1923 and paid by instalments as she was unable to afford an annual subscription.

Con's story was repeated *ad finitum* in parliamentary speeches, in the Suffragette-controlled media and also in the press thanks to her family's position as part of the aristocracy, her brother Victor's role in the House of Lords, and her grandfather's reputation as a respected novelist. *Prisons and Prisoners* was well received and sold over 3,000 copies in the first couple of weeks.

Writing to *The Times* on 30 April 1912, Con spoke of how 'the strain [of forced feeding] produced enlargement of the heart and abnormal conditions of that organ from which up to the present it has not yet recovered.' It was shortly after writing this letter that she'd suffered her near fatal stroke.

Dr Mary Gordon, the psychologist and the first prison inspector in England, described what had taken place by saying 'Such spiritual upheavals are always irrational, and irrational human types are swept into them as high priests. Con was seized and used. She was both flame and burnt offering.'

Writing in *Final Burning of Boats*, Ethel Smyth wrote:

Man, after war, who, when nothing but winning women's support at elections was in question, had glibly voiced our claims, would cast his promises to the winds when the hour struck for effective action; displaying the same stupidity, treachery, obstinacy, conceit and hypocrisy that had begotten and was now feeding militancy. 'Sex war indeed,' cries Constance Lytton 'is *this* not sex war? It is sex *peace* that we want!'

Another of Con's causes was a woman called Rachel Peace, also known as Jane Short. She was born in the early 1880s and was an embroideress before joining the women's suffrage movement. Having already suffered several breakdowns prior to joining the Suffragettes, her life was not so fortunate during her fourth imprisonment at Holloway. On 4 October 1913, she was imprisoned for eighteen months with hard labour after being arrested along with another Suffragette near the scene of a fire at an unoccupied mansion in Hampton, Surrey. Rachel was seen as a potential arsonist and her companion, Mary Richardson, was out of prison under the Cat and Mouse Act. Rachel Peace's picture had been taken as part of the surveillance images collected while exercising in the yard and written on the back of her image was the name 'Jane Short', the alias used by Peace. Like other Suffragettes before her, Rachel undertook a period of prolonged hunger striking. The prison doctor in return force fed her three times a day and Rachel feared 'I should go mad...old distressing symptoms have re-appeared. I have frightful dreams and am struggling with mad people half the night.' Rachel Peace was one of the last women to be force fed in prison and was apparently made an example of by the Home Office, who refused to release her under the Cat and Mouse Act. Unfortunately for Rachel, these fears became true when she 'lost her reason' in prison and required care within asylums after being released. Her case was widely publicised in various circles and the care she received within these asylums was funded by Con, who was terribly aware of the price that Rachel had paid, right up until her own death.

The Prisoners (Temporary Discharge for Ill Health) Act was passed in 1913 by Asquith's government. The Act, more commonly known as the Cat and Mouse Act, was put through specifically to deal with Suffragettes who were hunger striking in prison and whose experiences were in turn leading to public outcries across the country. The Act was designed to counteract these outcries by releasing any prisoners whose health was affected by force feeding for a short time and then, once their health had recovered, the prisoners were re-arrested and taken back to prison to serve the rest of their time. The nickname came from domestic cat's habits of playing with their prey, torturing it before allowing it to escape and then recapturing it again a number of times before finally killing it. Research suggests that the Act did very little to deter any activities with the Suffragettes and within a short space of the time the outbreak of the First World War led to the Suffragettes ceasing their militant actions in order to offer their support for the war effort.

In *Female Pipings of Eden*, Ethel Smyth described the Cat and Mouse Act as something

> Of which the murderous, cowardly, pseudo humane refinement is to my mind more revolting than any torture invented in the Middle Ages, was now in full swing. The authorities dared not let the women die, so would release them, sometimes half dead, to be re-arrested as soon as they were judged fit to serve the remainder of their sentence. Whereupon the whole hideous business would begin again, the idea being that by degrees bodies and wills would be broken past mending. How a group of civilised Christian men could lend themselves to this proceeding rather than perform a simple act of justice already fifty years overdue is inconceivable.

In 1913 Emily Davison, who had been imprisoned a grand total of eight times during her suffrage career, stressed that the perfect militant warrior 'will sacrifice all...to win the Pearl of Freedom for her sex'. Daisy Dorothea Solomon also saw her prison life as a 'baptism to work for the uplifting of womanhood'. Meanwhile, Kathleen Emerson wrote down her feelings on prison life, which were almost certainly shared by Con, in a poem that was subsequently published in the *Holloway Jingles*:

THE WOMEN IN PRISON
Oh, Holloway, grim Holloway,
With grey forbidding towers!
Stern are they walls, but sterner still
Is Woman's free, unconquered will.
And though to-day and yesterday
Brought long and lonely hours,
Those hours spent in captivity
Are stepping stones to liberty.

Con's friend Dr Alice Ker, with whom she stayed the night before she morphed into Jane Warton, also wrote a poem for *Holloway Jingles*, set to the tune of 'Annie Laurie':

Newington Butts were lively
    When sessions time fell due
For there sat Justice Lawrie,
    With twelve men good and true:
And sat to sentence me-
    And except for Justice Lawrie,
I'd be far away and free.

The lies piled up like snow drifts,
    The women's case looked wan;
Their answers were the bravest
    That e'er judge frowned upon:
And a biased judge was he-
    And except for Justice Lawrie,
I'd be far away and free.

Hear the Jew as witness lying,
    Measuring damages in feet;

And to hear the owner sighing,
    When it proves too much is sweet.
And all the world can see,
    That except for Justice Lawrie,
I'd be far away and free.

In contrast to publications such as Emmeline Pankhurst's *The Importance of the Vote* were texts such as physician Almroth Wright's *The Unexpurgated Case Against Woman Suffrage*, in which he states emphatically that 'no doctor can ever lose sight of the fact that the mind of a woman is always threatened with danger from the reverberations of her physiological emergencies…' It was thought that by giving women the vote this would not only mar those gifts but, in the views of anti-suffrage members such as Mary Augusta Ward, one of the founders of the National League for Opposing Woman Suffrage, it would increase 'the violent and excitable element in politics,' and arise a 'sex feeling and sex antogonism'. This in turn would impart 'the calm and practical discussion of great questions impossible'.

There were fears in a number of anti-suffrage communities that if women entered politics they might ignore their duties as wives and mothers and neglect their children etc. Emmeline Pankhurst responded to these arguments by saying that 'rearing and training of children...are the things that interest women. Politics have nothing to do with these things and therefore politics do not concern women.' She pointed out that laws determine 'how women are to live in marriage, how their children are to be trained and educated and what the future of their children is to be.'

Even though she was now an invalid, Con still managed to write the occasional piece for *Votes for Women*, such as this article about what a difference having the vote would make:

One cannot divine, shut up as I am from ill-health and scarcely able to read, how the vote would most significantly change the world were all women enfranchised on equal terms with men. In various countries the wants of women are different, but no doubt there would be a great substratum that would work the same anywhere. Honour for women, welfare for children; cleanliness, healthiness, morality for men, women and children. These are some of the chief aims of women, but what giant achievement they call up! The White Slave Traffic stopped, the horrors of syphilitic disease put an end to, the unprotected mothers defended by law, the prison, workhouse, and doss house abolished or transformed past recognition, the dwelling houses where women and families spend their life pulled down and replaced by healthy homes, the bars in education removed, the doors that are shut to women in nearly every walk of life thrown open. And through these changes there is a great light which shines from the dawning of a happier time – the greater freedom of the human race.

In 1914 Con wrote to Mr George Lansbury, a radical liberal, supporter of women's suffrage and later leader of the Labour Party, saying that she was pleased he was working for the suffrage movement and thanking his wife for the kind message – Con had been in bed since the end of April and it was now July – but that she was getting much better. Ethel Smyth wrote in *Final Burning of Boats* of Mr Lansbury that he

> ... was a great champion of women's suffrage, and was, I fancy, as sincere about it as any politician can be about anything. Anyhow he advocated militancy, went to prison, refused to sign a promise to mend his ways and faced the hunger strike. But whereas Gandhi stuck it till he gained his point after a day

or two, Mr Lansbury gave the required undertaking and was set free; the moral of which is that whereas the vote affected women only, half the Untouchables are of Gandhi's own sex.

This period in her life had been difficult for Con. She had tried to recover from the forced feeding, but her health had failed her and she was unable to serve the suffrage cause as much as she had wanted to. However, she had been able to use the time constructively to produce *Prisons and Prisoners* and must have been extremely proud of how it was received and the way it exposed the horrors of prison life for the Suffragettes at the time.

Chapter 7

Marie Stopes' Birth Control Clinic Improvements and Con's Final Years, 1914-1923

Con was very ill during June 1914, with only her mother allowed in to see her. Olive Schreiner mentioned in one of her letters that she was going to watch the Women's Deputation to the King through the streets of London and anticipated that the mounted police would stop the deputation long before it reached Buckingham Palace. Con would have been devastated to have missed this event.

When the First World War broke out, Con's thoughts turned straight away to her beloved Aunt T, whose son was going to fight:

> You have all my reverent sympathy. I think of you incessantly and of Edith. To think that a European war should have broken out when scarcely any of the countries wanted war, all in a moment! I am so glad that you and Edith can be together; she will comfort you as no other woman can, and she is strong and sensible, however great her distress.

Meanwhile, Con kept in touch with her Suffragette friends and when writing to Adela on 29 July 1915, she relayed some of her latest news:

> Annie Kenney came down a little while ago and was her most dear self. She told me about the home Mrs Pankhurst is starting for little babes who are illegitimately born and whose mothers

have either died or cannot care for them. Mrs Lawrence has been down twice lately. The second time she brought a thrilling lady – an American she had got to know on her American tour – Miss Madeleine Doty. She is a Prison Commissioner in America...Miss Doty has seen the Little Commonwealth [a community in Dorset for delinquent children, presided over by Homer Lane] and is hugely appreciative of it; says nothing in America is as good as that.

It was during this period, while Con was back living with her elderly mother at Homewood, that they were also accompanied by what her sister called 'a most peculiar set of servants who shout and sing all day'. Con tended to spend most days in her room, which family members felt smelled of flannel sheets and dog. Her nephews and nieces who visited remembered her peeling grapes and feeding them to her Pekingese while she talked to her visitors. On good days, she resumed her former interest in cleaning around the house and polishing things with Brasso. Con also resumed her old hobby of Japanese flower arranging, with her art on display in the dining room at Homewood. The flowers would be kept in flat pans intermixed with twigs and stones, which according to Con was preferred to the 'old long-established English fashion of massing together in a vase,' saying that 'To the Japanese, every flower has its meaning'.

Having read a poem celebrating Edith Cavell, the British nurse who had been shot for helping soldiers to escape from Belgium, she wrote to Adela:

As I understand Nurse Cavell, she deliberately helped her countrymen or the Allies to get away from Belgium to their different countries – the men of course to fight if they were able. Who would not have done this, on either side, if they could? And it was patriotism in her that strengthened her to do it. But it was something beyond patriotism that made her say to those who killed her, 'I must bear no malice in my heart.'

Throughout 1916, Con's sister Betty was still pursuing the women's suffrage cause. She had communicated with people such as Lord Northcliffe, the British newspaper and publishing magnate who owned the *Daily Mail*, who had suggested to Betty that there was still no interest in women suffrage, despite his asking several women their opinion on the matter. However, he did suggest that she should set up a public meeting on the subject to gauge further interest. Later that year, Mrs Henry Fawcett, leader of the National Women's Union, considered that legislation must be earned during the war if women were to have their share in dealing with reconstruction afterwards.

On 6 February 1918, four years after the publication of *Prisons and Prisoners*, Con marked in one of her notebooks a very important date in terms of women's suffrage: 'By the Representation of the People Act, about 6,000,000 women of 30 years of age and over obtained the Parliamentary Vote.' The vote had finally been granted to women, although only to those over 30, who were householders or wives of householders, occupiers of property with a £5 annual value, or were university graduates. This would have pleased Con to a certain extent during her invalid years at Homewood, after her active period as a Suffragette was over. She was invited to a suffrage celebration in the Royal Albert Hall but unfortunately was too ill to attend. Although the step forward was small in terms of women's suffrage, it was still an important one. During the war, the Suffragettes had turned their efforts temporarily towards assisting the war effort, but their cause had not been forgotten. The new franchise was not a fair settlement, however, as many women who had worked so hard during the war in hospitals and factories were still excluded from voting. Sadly, it was not until after Con's death, in 1928, that the full franchise was granted to women, meaning they would have the same rights as men.

Although one of Con's causes, women's suffrage, had been (partially) resolved, her quest for prison reform was still ongoing. Between 1915 and 1919, Dr Mary Gordon wrote to Con from Sheffield Terrace in Kensington. As well as hoping that her hand was getting better following her stroke, she reported that in the meantime, nothing was happening in the prisons; the same women were still interred and that only war work was being done. She later wrote that she was still running the Inebriate Acts Department single-handedly and that she too had acquired a Pekingese puppy of a strong character. Dr Gordon remarked that there were tales going around of internal quarrels within the WSPU, something that at one time would have been thought impossible.

Both Mary Gordon and Con had a strong interest in prison reform and they had discussed how there was only one real punishment within all the prison systems, which was the loss of liberty. Mary felt that imprisonment was a terrible thing, and although the number of incurables was limited, the current system was not the right method for educating or detaining criminals, and of these criminals the only ones that she could not 'understand' were the poisoners.

A further letter from Mary Gordon appears to have caused offence, when she recommended a certain Mrs Savill, an alternative practitioner, might come to see Con for an £8 or £10 fee. Mrs Savill would be able to suggest electrical treatment that Con's nurse could then continue at home once shown how. Another letter written a week later suggests a misunderstanding regarding Mrs Savill and Con's health. Dr Gordon reiterated that her friend's health was not a simple case and that she should regularly be seeing a specialist twice a year. She explained that her health should not be seen as an unnecessary trouble or expense, and that it would be a good thing if her condition were to be made comfortable. Dr Gordon wondered if Con's nerves need re-educating and if her ill health may be related to St Vitus Dance, also known as Sydenham's Chorea, a disorder that causes jerking of the face, hands and feet thought to be caused by the streptococcal infection and acute rheumatic fever.

On 29 August 1919, Olive Schreiner wrote to Joan Hogson saying:

> I've just had a long letter from my dear friend Lady Constance Lytton. I don't know if you knew her in the suffrage days. She's one of the most beautiful women souls the Gods ever made. She has to undergo a great operation in two months. For 25 years she & her cousin Adela Smith have been my two closest friends. In this dark time one clings so to the thought of these great selfless souls; there's nothing in life matters much but love.

Con was worried about the operation and wrote to Adela:

> If it should happen I should not survive, I am happy to die. If, as many people believe, we step into a higher life, but are again with loved companions who have died before, then it will be very good. If death is the end and we do not consciously live again, it is still good. Death to me is a gentle lover, and kind to all that has been life, whether he bridges different stages or is the end of all consciousness. I am so tired of life, I should like to be taken in his sheltering arms and have an end. So I see three roads, as it were, of which by far the most likely is that I shall live on as usual. But I don't feel sad about it. I have long hoped to die, and I've seen this possible road, I have felt most wonderfully happy. Of late years I have seen and felt much of the sad side of death – the separation from those we love. Now I can see the joyful side – the release from bodily ills – and it is restful beyond all words.

In September that year, Con underwent surgery to remove an internal cyst. When he operated, Dr Aldrich Blake had found that the cyst was bigger than expected – roughly the size of a head or football – and subsequently a few days later reviewed the report on the cyst: it was not malignant or cancerous and should not reoccur. Olive Schreiner, writing from Porchester Place in London, hoped that Con would be in less pain now that the cyst had been removed.

Con wrote to Annie Kenney in 1920, after losing touch during the First World War, to congratulate her on her marriage and to ask if she could visit Homewood. Like most of the other Suffragettes, Con had trouble adjusting to Annie's new surname, Taylor, and interestingly, many of Christabel Pankhurst's letters were addressed to 'Annie Kenney Taylor' or 'A.K. Taylor'. When Con's sister Betty also wrote to Annie after the marriage, the letter began with, 'My dear Mrs Taylor (I should like to call you Annie Kenney?)'

Later, in July 1920, Con sent Annie a brooch of white sapphires as a gift, saying that although it was not worth much in cost, it meant a lot in sentimental value as she always wore it above her hunger strike medal. Con loved children and was so pleased to hear of Annie's pregnancy 'Oh! How happy I am to think you have already a secret!' Annie was 41 when her baby was born and, having always believed that having children was part of a woman's calling, she now made Warwick, her only child, a central part of her life.

On 25 February 1921, Con wrote to Marie Stopes in response to her request to use Con's name as a patron for her 'Mother's Clinic' on Marlborough Road in Upper Holloway. Con said that she would do all she could to assist but was still invalided following her stroke and feared that she would be of little help, bar writing to people. Nevertheless, she wished the clinic every success, saying that she admired Marie and had read a great number of her books and pamphlets during her suffrage days. She also said she would send for Marie's book, *Married Love*.

Marie Stopes was seen as a sexual revolutionary who pioneered the formation of birth control clinics in working-class areas and paved the way for modern family planning. The introduction to her book states 'More than ever today are happy homes needed. It is my hope that this book may serve the State by adding to their number. Its object is to increase the joys of marriage, and to show how much sorrow may be avoided.' It contained controversial content for the time, including discussions on how to have great sex and that marriage should be a shared partnership.

Marie enlisted the support of prominent figures as patrons for her cause such as Charlotte Despard and Margaret Ashton (both ladies with an interest in children's welfare), as well as Con, for her first clinic. There is no indication, however, that Con shared Stopes' thoughts on eugenics and racial purity.

Con was invited to the opening of the clinic on 17 March but was forced to decline due to her health. Con was very enthusiastic about Stopes' book, *Married Love*, saying it was the kind of book she longed to be written, but was do much better. She was also impressed by the list of other patrons, although the only ones she knew personally were Sir Malcom Maurice (her father's former doctor) and Mrs Despard. In April Con was sent a ticket to attend a meeting at Queen's Hall on the subject of constructive birth control, and although she thought the subject was a sound principle to be put forward, she unfortunately needed to return the ticket as she was still very unwell. However, she felt that birth control might make great headway in the next five to ten years.

Later, in May, Con wrote to newspapers such as *The Times*, the *Morning Post*, the *Daily Mail* and *The Mirror* in support of Marie Stopes as there had been some disagreement against her work published in the press. As a result, Con started receiving post in response to her support, including one from a 'madman'. Marie invited Con to become Vice President, alongside others including Mrs Pethick-Lawrence, of an organisation she proposed to set up called the Society for Constructive Birth Control and Racial Progress.

The society believed that 'The haphazard production of children by ignorant, coerced, or diseased mothers is profoundly detrimental to the race' and that 'Many men and women should be prevented from procreating at all, because of their individual ill-health, or the diseased and degenerate nature of the offspring that they may be expected to produce.' Her clinics were set up in poor areas, such as the first one in Holloway, which is still running today.

Con sent books to her new friend Marie Stopes, such as the *Lytton Treasury*, which featured selections made by Alfred Broadbent from the poems of Robert, Earl of Lytton. On the inside cover she wrote, 'To Dr Marie Stopes, with great admiration and affection'.

The letters between the two ladies show genuine warmth in the relationship that was developing. In July 1921, Con wrote to her friend and told her how her brother, Lord Lytton, was impressed with *Married Love* and wished to offer his assistance if he could. She hoped to visit Marie's new clinic in the autumn and to arrange a time when both Marie and her husband, Humphrey Verden Roe (also a co-founder of the clinic), would be there, although Con would have to sit downstairs as she became out of breath easily when walking. Marie sent Con a card inviting her to a meeting on 13 October, which Con planned to accept and bring along her sister Betty Balfour, who was herself a mother of six and an influencer in women's work. Con admitted that she might not be able to watch much of the meeting due to her condition, but she could wait outside if needed and Betty would update her. Fortunately, Con did manage to attend and thought the lecture was 'first rate'.

On 7 December Con had been in bed since Armistice Day (11 November) and as such had to decline another meeting with Marie Stopes. By Christmas 1921, Con wrote to Marie informing her that she had just heard that her sister Emily Lutyens had given a copy of *Married Love* to her daughter, who had recently married, and who had enjoyed reading it.

Marie Stopes invited Con to a banquet at the Hotel Cecil on 12 April 1922, but Con once again had to decline as she was too ill and because her breathlessness was now affecting her ability to speak. Con said that she would try to distribute some cards that Marie had sent her for the meeting of 16 March, but feared she did not know enough people. Marie had complemented her actions as a Suffragette, but Con dismissed these achievements, saying that other women had done greater things or suffered for the cause, particularly Rachel Peace, who had gone mad through forced feeding and was still mad as a result.

Con hoped that she might be able go to the clinic in the spring and explained to Marie how she was visiting a wonderful psychoanalyst called Homer Lane, who believed that by Christmas time she would be on the road to good health. This was hugely exciting for Con as she had felt more dead than alive for the least ten years of her life. The Lytton family had a strange association with the American Homer Lane. To some he was an abusive charlatan who practised psychoanalysis, but the Lyttons found him charismatic and he soon became Con's guru physician after he had treated one of her brothers.

Lane was the superintendent of a co-educational community in Dorset called the Little Commonwealth, between 1913 and 1918. Established by George Montagu, who later became the Earl of Sandwich, Homer Lane was recruited by the management committee that Montagu had set up to oversee the project as a result of his management work with the Ford Boys Republic in America. It accommodated children aged from a few months to 19 years of age, with those who were over 13 tending to be there as they were categorised as delinquent. During this time, he pioneered group therapy and shared responsibility. Lane claimed to be able to cure his citizens by the mere act of living with them. Some of the methods used at the Little Commonwealth were sure to have been replicated during his time as a psychotherapist. His work at the Little Commonwealth came to a sudden end in December 1917 when two of the young female citizens claimed that Lane had had immoral relations with them. The two 16-year-olds accused him of sexually assaulting them, and one reported her allegations to the police. A Home Office enquiry was opened to investigate the case, and Lane was removed as superintendent, and the school was closed in the summer of 1918. Historian Lucy Dalap has suggested that the allegations against Homer Lane were the 'first well-documented case of alleged institutional abuse in Britain'. Earl Lytton was part of the managing committee of the Little Commonwealth, and he continued to endorse Lane saying that:

> Promiscuous misconduct of the kind suggested could only be committed by a man who was super sexual and morbidly unnatural. There are such men, but Mr Lane is not one of them. If he were, we should have to admit that he was also a super hypocrite...and that all of us who have known him intimately for many years have been *completely duped* as to his character.

After the Little Commonwealth closed in 1918, Lane took up psychoanalysis at a private practice in London, treating patients via close observation and his own forceful personality. Con wrote to Jessie, Annie Kenney's sister, and told her that she was visiting a therapist who was easing her conditions 'It seems like a miracle after being for ten years half dead'.

Writing at the end of May 1922, Con stated that she had asked her sister Emily to arrange for Lane to meet her during a trip to the dentist in London. She was interested in the new doctrines of psychoanalysis and this one, Laneism, was one that she felt she could 'go in for'. She had been reading about the subject for the past two to three years, but did not understand how the self-taught ill health applied in her case as she had 'found her feet' in the Votes for Women movement and had made so many new friends who made her happy. However, her stroke had rendered her almost completely incapacitated and she was forced to live and rely upon her relations, whom she felt disapproved of her 'work', and as such, she was cut off from the world that made her happy and desperately hoped that Lane would help her to find a way out.

Lane was a particularly attractive man and there was no doubt that Con was obsessed with him. After she became a patient of his, Lane's name came up in nearly every single letter she wrote to her friends and family. On 17 October 1922, she wrote to her brother Victor, another devotee and ex-patient of Lane's, saying, 'I can think of nothing but Laneisms from week to week, my mind and whole self are steeped in it.' Con had admitted that Lane was the nearest thing to an angel she had ever seen, which suggests that she may have been in love with him. John Ponsonby had previously had the effect of bringing her back to life, and Con likewise wrote of Lane that, 'He has made me live again and content whether with life or death, paralysis or health.'

Lane's methods as a psychoanalyst were just as controversial as those he used at the Little Commonwealth. During his sessions with Con, he disregarded the physical evidence for her health conditions and instead blamed the illness on her antics as a Suffragette, blaming both herself and the WSPU. Lane tried to convince Con that her stroke was a punishment, that her subconscious was against suffragettism and had taken revenge on her body through a stroke. Con was then left wondering what part of suffragettism her sub-consciousness disliked. She had argued with Lane about the Women's Movement, as he believed that all the chief leaders, such as Mrs Pethick-Lawrence, Mrs Pankhurst and Miss Annie Kenney, had suffered great sorrow before they took up militancy and also believed that their militant tactics were wrong. Some of these discussions about her friends made Con angry. However, she was beginning to see some improvements where she could lift her right hand up to the top of her head and she found it easier to get up and down the stairs.

Today we may consider Lane's interpretations on the fight for women's suffrage as highly suspect, and that he was a dangerous quack with poor medical knowledge, having completely misdiagnosed the early signs of Con's heart failure. Her symptoms included swelling in both feet and legs, a distended stomach that had trouble digesting food and the clearly visible veins in her paralysed right hand. Con was soothed by both his authority and assurance, and was keen to follow his advice that she should leave Homewood and move to London so that she could have extra sessions with him and thus lead to a quicker improvement in her health. She allowed Lane to read all her letters and frequently copied items because she thought they would interest him, or be a tribute to his psychology.

Writing to Betty in mid-September 1922, Con discussed her busy day travelling around London, seeing her Aunt T, Lane, and then shopping afterwards. Her letter almost sounds like the old days when she was busy as a Suffragette. Betty had suggested that she try her hand at writing again, but Con dismissed the idea saying that she did not have enough time to do so and the results would be poor anyhow. In mid-October, Lane had gone away for a week's holiday to a friend's house near Paris, with Con's approval. She had wanted to take some time off from her appointments with him as her correspondence was piling up and all she could think of, day and night, were her meetings. She pointed out that because she was feeling so much better, missing a few sessions would not be an issue in her opinion, but that she would stick to him like a leech otherwise.

Con regularly sent books, newspaper cuttings and pamphlets to her brother Victor on various subjects, including birth control, as well as a copy of her friend Dr Mary Gordon's *Penal Discipline*. Dr Mary Gordon had told her that she believed the current system was dead and created a criminal class that directly fostered recidivism. Other books that Con had eagerly read on the subject and enthused about in her letters included *English Local Government: English Prisons Under Local Government* by Sydney Webbs, with a preface by Bernard Shaw, and *English Prisons Today*, a report by The Prison System Enquiry Committee established by The Executive of the Labour Research Department. She was also interested in the League of Nations Union, which promoted international justice, collective security and permanent peace based on the ideals of the League of Nations. Indeed, she had been keen to hold a meeting on their behalf earlier in the year at the big hall in Knebworth.

In October 1922, Con was pleased to hear that a fellow Suffragette who had also been forcibly fed, Mary Richardson, was standing as a Labour candidate for Acton, in Middlesex, where she received 26 percent of the vote against a successful Conservative candidate. In the same month, an acquaintance of Con's, George Blackshaw, stole money from Marie Stopes after befriending her by using Con's name. She pleaded with Marie to let her know how much Blackshaw owed her and received a letter from the police at the same time as one from Marie to say that he had been convicted for the sixth time. Con wrote to him, asking him to visit her, and that she would even pay for his fare, but she feared that he would not come. In her eyes it was a pity that he continued to defraud people and spend his time in and out of prison; she clearly wished she could do more to help reform him.

In December, Con asked Marie if they could meet in London as she had promised her nephew Robert Lutyens a short article on birth control for a February edition of *The Herald*. If Marie was unavailable, Con asked whether she could send her a copy of the article for approval before it was published. In February 1923 Con wrote again to Marie regarding the libel lawsuit against Dr Halliday Sutherland. Con believed the publicity of birth control would do some good and that it would be terrible for women and the next generation if there was no interference. Although Marie lost her case, she decided to appeal, with Con writing letters to various people in the hope that they might be able to assist.

At the start of January 1923, Con wrote to Victor to tell him how her friend Dr Mary Gordon had visited her and stayed the night. They had both discussed her plans for moving away from Homewood and into London, where she could receive more sessions with Lane and escape 'the clutches of her mother'. Dr Gordon disagreed with the plan and said that it would be cruel of her to leave, and that she had also had a conversation with Edith, who had told Con that Mary was a very wise woman. Con was dismayed and torn as to what to do. Her instinct told her to give up her plans, but she felt that she would end up in a grave if she stayed and was unhelpful to her mother. However, she had thought Edith was coming around to the idea. Con wished to know what her siblings would do if they were in her place, and although she knew that they had managed to leave home and marry etc., her circumstances were quite different. Her plan was to go to London, lead her own life, see her friends, and get better from her 'bodily and mentally' ills through visits to her psychoanalyst Homer Lane. She hoped that Victor, Betty, Neville and Emily would each offer up their own opinion on the subject, and then she would discuss the responses with their mother. Con reiterated Lane's thoughts that if she could move to London, his work would be twice as effective because returning to Homewood and her mother after each session was potentially undoing his good work. All her siblings agreed about the plan, although they knew it would be hard for Edith to let go. The name John Ponsonby, the man Con had wanted to marry, had cropped up again in a letter from Victor, and Con felt that the things he said of him were 'delightful and dreamy'.

Victor had written to Edith and advised her to meet Homer Lane herself. He wanted Edith to hide her feelings from Con as otherwise she would fret about her mother and the treatment would not work. He too believed that Edith was 'intimately connected' with Con's illness, but wanted to reassure his mother that Con, once better, would not take up another 'tiresome cause'. He reiterated that Con was torn between her love for her mother and her desire to be healthy and happy once again. Later, at the end of February, Victor was pleased to tell Con that the council in Calcutta had passed women's suffrage in their municipal elections in Bengal.

In late January, Edith did indeed meet Homer Lane. Con described how Edith fell into his arms (metaphorically speaking) and appeared to enjoy his company. Con felt that Edith had realised everyone was on the same page about her (Con's) situation and that they were keen for her to carry out her plan. She had agreed to live with a companion in her new rooms, and the girl in question was to be the daughter of Victor's gardener, who could also type and do shorthand. However, Con was frequently worried about money and how to pay for her sessions with Homer Lane. Victor, currently living in Government House, Calcutta, as Governor of Bengal, offered to pay. Her mother also offered to double her income and Lane had mentioned giving her a season ticket and not taking payment. However, she wanted to do things honestly, scrimping and saving her money to be able to pay him, including using her birthday money of £5 from Edith. She attempted to write articles again for three weeks but struggled to get her words out on paper, saying her work was like the writing of a child and that it gave her headaches, with her brain feeling like it was on fire. The inability to write the article she had promised Robert Lutyens wounded her vanity somewhat. She did, however, continue to work on her cookbook of different nations' plain foods, asking Victor to obtain a recipe on how to make chapattis, both the common ones and a finer, crisper kind.

Letters between Homewood and India took time to travel and would often 'cross in the post'. Victor felt that once Con was well again, she might move back to live with Edith and be able to swap roles and care for her. Everyone in the family was secretly worried that Con was not fit to live in London alone; what if she had another attack? If she did, and no one was with her, it might prove fatal. However, the family was reconciled to Con's plan and wanted to leave the responsibility of curing and providing care for Con to Homer Lane.

Towards the end of February, Con had an interview with her publishers, Heinemann, regarding her cookery book. She reported to Victor that she was feeling remarkably better and that she could get around London on her own but was not yet recovered from her paralysis and would be uncomfortable staying with friends or relatives in town. Her mother had increased her allowance, meaning everything was now affordable. In the meantime, Con visited 'her two prisoners', as she liked to refer to them (sadly their names remain unknown); her family thought of them as more of her 'lost causes', but Con referenced them as interesting, lovable beings.

In March, Con reported that she had received a recipe from the Master of the Queen's Household, Sir Derek Keppel, and, through Ned Lutyens, a dish from Queen Victoria's still room. However, because she still had to wait for the other recipes to come from abroad, her cookery book would not be published until autumn. As such she thought she might bring out a book of collated ballads, songs and rhymes later in the spring, and although nothing need be composed by her, it would bring in a little bit of extra money.

A week later Con eagerly wrote to Victor telling him of how her sister Emily had visited Homewood and offered her a room in her office of *The Star*, at 6 Tavistock Square. Emily edited the theosophical journal of the *Herald Star* from here when she was not touring the country lecturing on theosophical matters or surrogate parenting Krishnamurti. Emily did not require Con to pay rent, and there would be several other women living there to keep an eye on her, as well as two dogs, a cat and two-month-old kittens for company. Con accepted, with her mother's approval, and Lane also approved of the idea, declaring it was the same room that he had had when the Little Commonwealth had broken up. Two days later Con went shopping in London with her mother's maid to pick up a few 'necessities', as Edith did not want her to take anything from Homewood. While she was in town, she met Edith who took her to Tavistock Square to meet everyone and inspect the room.

A few days later Betty came to visit Con, concerned that she was giving her own money away to ex-prisoners and fearing that she was becoming unreliable. Con was offended; she had lent money, not given it away, to her ex-prisoner friends who were, in her eyes, short of money through no fault of their own, such as from business deals that had gone wrong. Con had recommended one of these ex-prisoners to Victor for a position in one of his Indian prisons. Con had known the man since the summer of 1922, and described him as being tall, self-possessed, well-educated and both the editors and police spoke well of him. He had written articles on prison reform, having been imprisoned for theft, but had no plans to go back there. Con was worried about him as it was said that the 'European gang of thieves' (a quote from her letter of 5 February 1923), was trying to get him for their own devices when he was released from prison.

By 19 March 1923 Con had moved into 6 Tavistock Square. Her mother had paid for all the necessary furnishings and Con was pleased to find a splendid writing table in situ and the bathroom opposite her room. The move had exerted her, though, leaving her feeling helplessly bad with breathlessness. In previous days, her excitement and going out shopping had necessitated a ransack through her drug cupboard, leading her to take salvolatile, spirits of chloroform etc. She was planning to see Lane every other day and to return to Homewood at weekends. She returned for Easter and began reading her old letters between herself and John Ponsonby, which in turn made her feel unwell with heart palpitations, breathlessness, sleeplessness and lack of hunger. When she told Lane of this, he recommended that rather than putting these thoughts and memories aside, she should have it all out with Maggie Ponsonby, John's sister. Con mentioned to Victor in a letter that she had given herself to John, that he could ask of her whatever he chose and that she still loved her mother despite the fact that Edith was against her marrying John and having children. Lane had told Con that the John Ponsonby business was the most upsetting part of her life and that she needed to learn to live with it.

Meanwhile, Victor was still writing to Con thinking that she was still resisting the move and, as such, Betty decided to cable him with the news that Con had already been in London for four weeks and was seeing an improvement in her condition. However, this improvement was short-lived and in early April, Con noticed that the veins in her right hand had become very visible and both her feet and legs were swollen. When she mentioned this to Lane, he said it was the circulation coming back into her paralysed side. Around the same time, Victor sent his wife Pamela back to Homewood so that she could look after and cheer up Edith.

In many eyes, there were two key men in Con's life, John Ponsonby and Homer Lane, who both accelerated her depressions and, in Homer Lane's case, encouraged, although perhaps not intentionally, the deterioration of her health. Each man represented freedom: John from spinsterhood and Homer from her paralysis, and both had the potential to help Con get away from her mother. The most fulfilling experience of freedom she had, however, was being a member of the WSPU.

Towards the end of April 1923, Con reported that she still was not feeling quite right; her feet, legs and stomach were swollen beyond any previous occasions, but her hand and arm on the paralysed side were improving daily. When she returned to London it would be to new accommodation, because although she loved being at Tavistock Square, it was embarrassing passing people in the corridor to use the bathroom when she felt ill.

On 1 May Betty wrote to Con saying that Homer Lane had accused her of playing at recovery and insisted that if she wanted to get better then she must move to quarters that had been prepared for her and take on Lane's treatment. Betty said that Con must swallow her pride and recommended that she put herself in his hands. She appealed to Con's altruistic and self-sacrificing nature, pleading with her not to agree for her own sake but to help advance Lane's career, saying that:

> You will be a mine of wealth to him…Every day you delay you are putting off his reward. I left him treading on air, I felt as if I had held up a bright torch to prisoners in a pit, promising them light, freedom, safety. If you don't agree to put yourself into his hands it is as if you were snatching the torch and putting it out.

Con was unable to resist this appeal and agreed to put herself entirely in Lane's hands. In one of her last letters, she mentioned feeling more and more ill, and had symptoms of jaundice. There was talk between her and Lane of becoming his partner or debtor, as she still had money concerns and did not wish to involve her family in such matters.

Twenty days later, after relocating to London and renting a flat in Paddington, Con died on Tuesday, 22 May 1923, aged just 54. The next day, Victor received a telegram from Pamela saying that Con was seriously ill in London. There was some confusion about advice that had been given, with Victor stating that he had not intended for Con to refuse to see a doctor about her symptoms. A further telegram then arrived confirming the sad news that Con had passed away, with Victor stuck in India and unable to comfort the rest of his family. He replied to Edith almost a month later in response to her letter describing the funeral. Neville had walked beside Edith during the cortege and Victor said it sounded perfectly arranged and how much Con would have liked the service. He was pleased to hear that many of her fellow workers attended.

Betty blamed Con's death on Lane, who instead privately blamed it on Edith. Betty explained the situation in a letter to her devastated brother, Victor, dated 3 July 1923.

> I feel fearfully disappointed and feel a glorious experiment has failed. Physiologically it is easy to explain her death...Lane so completely ignored the Dr's view of the case that I think he thought the family surrounding her made her ill. The grim thing still to me is that I believe Lane in his heart thinks her family killed her and that he never had a chance of getting her free from all hampering love...It is much more true to say Lane killed her – but I don't regret it – for like you, better to make the attempt and fail than see her a hopeless prisoner.

Although her spirit had been weakened by her 'imprisonment' at home with her mother, liberation from her family had proven to be too much for both Con's body and heart. She had strode out with the support of her brother and sister, resisted the advice of her mother and friend Dr Gordon, and succumbed to Lane's charlatan psychologies. She had taken a life-or-death decision in her belief that life at home was not worth living: 'My instinct is to do as mother wishes and give up living in London. At the same time I seem to know that my life here was in the grave and not vital or helpful to mother.' Once again, she was measuring her life in terms of its worth as a dutiful daughter. Reflecting on the prospect of death, Con declared:

> I'm quite glad to live and there seems much to be done. But I shall always be, I think, quite glad to die. Living on the whole I have a sad and painful thing and tho' with Lane...once could do many good and joy-making things still it will always remain a sad place, this world, through my spectacles, even if I myself am healthy and powerful.

These melancholy sentiments appeared in a letter Con wrote to her brother Victor, where she refused to allow him to pay the fees for Homer Lane's services. Once more Con was determined not to be a financial drain upon her family. Perhaps if she had accepted Victor's offer, she might have been able to enjoy some independence that would have given her autonomy and freedom.

After Con's death, Lane found himself in legal trouble. He was said to have had tremendous power over his patients and disciples and even accepted the gift of a motor car from a female patient. He called himself 'Daddy' and his patients were called 'pupils'. These pupils, such as the Viceroy of India (Victor Lytton), sat at his feet and confessed that they were happier and saner men because of his work. One pupil triggered his final chapter of working in Britain as a psychoanalyst. A well-off but highly neurotic woman had given him large gifts of money, which worried her father, who then complained to the Home Office that his daughter was in the clutches of an undesirable alien. Arrested in March 1925, Lane was expelled under the Aliens Act for failing to notify a change of address to the police. Deported to Paris due to a technical point, he died shortly after from typhoid and pneumonia.

Con's funeral was held at Knebworth Park on 28 May 1923, where a large gathering declared that she was 'made one with nature'. She was buried in the green, white and purple colours of the Suffragettes, and during the funeral, Emmeline Pethick-Lawrence placed a palm leaf on the casket. The accompanying statement read, 'Dearest comrade, you live always in the hearts of those who love you and you live forever in the future race which inherits the new freedom you gave your life to win.'

The first part of the ceremony took place in the parish church and was conducted by the Reverend C.E. Rainey, the rector of Knebworth. The fourteenth chapter of St John's Gospel was read by the young Lord Knebworth and the hymn 'Peace, Perfect Peace' was sung by the choristers. The casket containing Con's cremated ashes lay in the chancel during the service and was covered with a sheaf of white lilies. Shaped like a tiny coffin, the casket was borne to her final resting place by her brother Neville and Mr Raymond, the gardener of Knebworth Park, and was followed by an informal procession of both relatives and friends to the stone mausoleum, erected by Elizabeth Bulwer-Lytton in 1817. Following a short ceremony, her casket was placed upon the coffin of the late Earl Robert Bulwer-Lytton and the final benediction was read. By special request there were no flowers other than the sheaf of lilies and a small posy of pansies. The inscription on her headstone read: 'Endowed with a celestial sense of humour, boundless sympathy, and rare musical talent, she devoted the later years of her life to the political enfranchisement of women and sacrificed her health and talents in helping to bring victory to this cause.'

As well as the members of Con's family who attended her funeral, in amongst the large numbers of attendees could be seen women wearing badges depicting the old groups from the former suffrage movements, as well as people from different social classes; a reflection on the fact that Con had made many friends from all walks of life. Strangers Con had never met felt that her sufferings and sacrifice had been endured especially for them. One letter of condolence written by a woman after Con's death read: 'I never saw her...but, like many others, I feel today the same deep impulse of gratitude and love that I've felt in the dark days when she lay in prison for us.'

The *Women's Dreadnought* of 2 June 1923 wrote a tribute to Con saying:

> The death of Lady Constance Lytton removes one of the most heroic figures in the Suffragette Movement. Though suffering from chronic heart complaints, she endured four imprisonments and was twice a hunger-striker. She joined the

militant deputations to the House of Commons on February 24th 1909...Constance Lytton was no madcap plunging into the Suffrage Movement for excitement or notoriety. In spite of her aristocratic environment, she was already a democrat... [she] was a subscriber to the *Workers Dreadnought* from its first issue to the time of her death.

In response, the newspaper received the following letter a week later:

Dear Editor – I was deeply touched by your fine tribute to Constance Lytton or Lady Connie, as she was affectionately called at Knebworth, where everyone loved her. Her good work must continue. I will gladly keep up her subscription to the 'Dreadnought'. Kindly let me know the amount, and I will ask you to put it down in her name, if she were still alive. Yours faithfully Sepdekiaya Sufragulo, Welwyn Garden City.

In 1925, Con's sister Betty selected some of Con's correspondence to be put into a book called *Letters of Constance Lytton*. They were chosen from correspondence between her mother Edith; her Aunt T; Mrs Maria Earle, her cousin; Mrs Francis Smith; and Betty, her sister. Mrs Earle passed away in February 1925, just before the book was published, but had been keen to see these letters in print. Maurice Baring had also helped to choose the letters and advised on their selection and arrangement.

A letter from Mrs Coombe Tennant, the prison visitor, later printed in *Letters of Constance Lytton*, said that Con: 'Has a place in the historical story of Prison Reform, and that prisons to-day are different to what they would have been, had she not gone down into hell...I simply say she had a share in altering the world and shaping thought among women. Who could ask for a better epitaph?'

Maurice Baring, Con's gentleman friend who was perhaps more fond of her than John Ponsonby (the man she had hoped to marry), also wrote a description of Con's character to be included in the book, which encapsulated her perfectly:

The better the friend the more he hesitates to write. Her fastidious taste would have minded a wrong note in such a tribute, as much as a musician minds an unintentional discord; but her kind heart would at once have forgiven it, and she would have concealed the wince. She could laugh at anything without being unkind. She had a celestial sense of humour and infinite powers of appreciation. Her tolerance and her toleration were wonderful; nobody could make a purse out of a sow's ear when it was necessary to do so more deftly and more tactfully. Almost you were persuaded that it was silk.

She was quite unconscious of her gifts; she was cultivated and original and witty and talented, and she considered herself quite giftless. When her exquisite, sensitive, delicate nature reached the conviction that it was her duty to help social wrongs and evils, and to help to fight them in a particular way, she was at once faced with what meant the sacrifice of her life. She made the sacrifice, and it was of a kind that, whatever we may think of the cause that inspired it, or of the actions it entailed, there can be but one thing for us to do, and that is to bare the head in silence before her heroic courage and her sublime selflessness.

Her delicate frame was broken in the struggle, but her radiant spirit was unimpaired, and continued to give 'kindly light' until she died. She made one, we feel, with all happy, cheerful things; with fairy tales and cradle songs, the laughter of children and the toys of angels.

Many people must have said when they read of her death what Poor Jo in 'Bleak House' said about his benefactor: 'she wos werry good to me, she wos.' She would have laughed at any one quoting Dickens about her (an author she detested), but she would have enjoyed the fun of it, and she would have understood, and would have thought it quite right on the part of her old friend.

The *Women's Leader and the Common Cause* newspaper wrote on 26 June 1925:

> More important and of more lasting value is the picture drawn of Lady Constance Lytton herself, and the revelation of a character which was at once violent and gentle, passionately sympathetic and full of fun. No extracts can convey the impression which grew up from her own letters, her bits of self-revelation, her persistent driving force. Whatever the debate judgement on the whole may be, the part which Lady Con played seems wholly admirable, helpful and unwise; and the spirit in which she acted was that of a true saint. Her book *Prisons and Prisoners* drove the facts home and there is no doubt that her action had its results upon a sphere wider even than the great woman's movement she was upholding.

In 1930, Gerald Balfour, Con's brother-in-law, succeeded his brother Arthur as a peer after his brother's death and Betty became the Countess of Balfour. Betty had always had an interest in the occult and believed that just before the Second World War, she contacted Con through a seance. Betty described seeing 'A woman who passed to this life some time ago, seeming as if in some way in life she was a lonely person. She shows me prison clothes but she does not say what crime she committed…she says "prison gave me my freedom".'

Betty passed away in 1942 of a perforated duodenal ulcer, leaving Gerald bereft of a 'rare and radiant being'. Edith, their mother, had already passed away on 17 September 1936.

The reminisces interviews stored at the Women's Library at the LSE offer an insight into what those close to Con thought of her a little later in life, following the destruction of some of her letters after her death by her immediate family. Elizabeth Lutyens, the daughter of Con's sister Emily, said that her mother did not like the militant Suffragettes and that they had an unattractive side to them with their slogans and bra burning. Her mother had disapproved of her Aunt Con going against her class, where she behaved with great eccentricity and embarrassment to the family. Con had hurt Elizabeth's grandmother, Edith, by doing vulgar and militant things, and had had an unhappy love affair (presumably John Ponsonby) that was affected, she believed, by money, while her father had wanted her to stay at home. Elizabeth described Con as not being beautiful but having striking eyes and a rather large nose. She had tremendous vivacity, despite being a chronic invalid, with a very good figure, and her whole face would light up with her infectious laugh, lovely dark blue eyes, and dark hair that was inclined to curl. The interviews confirm that since she was a 7-month-old baby, Con had had a bad heart and that when she was invalided, her flannel sheets had to be kept very hot and she had a permanent nurse, Oram, who was of great character.

Lady Davinia Woodhouse, Con's niece, said that her aunt had made an error in becoming a militant Suffragette and that she was 'got hold of by them'. She believed it was a family trait to be led by strange people, although perhaps it may have been better than a dull life?

Meanwhile, Hermione Cobbold, another niece, described her Aunt Con as an invalid with a nurse to look after her, but a rather frail person with marvellous eyes. There were days when the children were not allowed in to see her because she was unwell, but on the days where she was well enough for visits, she became breathless quite quickly and spoke quietly. She wore her medals regularly and the children thought that she was marvellous. She had sympathy for children and would read their essays, listen to what they had to say and had a shelf of 'nic nacs', treasures, that she used to give away. Hermione went on to say that she thought Con's stroke had affected her mentality in the last year or so of her life, making her 'unbalanced', although not in an insane way, but that her judgement was not what it once was.

Lady Ann Lytton said of Con that she used to read fairy tales and made her believe in them. Con did not approve of prison, she said, but was a rebellious daughter, which was upsetting to her mother Edith. According to Ann, Aunt Con seemed to be the most un-militant person you could meet. She often made excuses for unpleasant people and refused to see the evil in them. Con could have been a professional pianist, said Ann, but was not allowed to be, which was quite exasperating. Ann described Con as having a marvellous sense of humour and someone who was always happy. She explained how when she was younger, Con was extremely smart and had beautiful handwriting.

The year 2023 marked 100 years since the death of Lady Constance Lytton, who today is generally remembered for her actions as Jane Warton, where she disguised herself as a working-class activist in order to experience and expose the prison system to show how inmates were treated differently depending on their social class. To commemorate her actions, women lay flowers at her resting place every International Women's Day, on 8 March. However, Con was not just interested in prison reform and women's suffrage, but also in folk dancing, flower arranging, Marie Stopes' contraception clinics and local causes. She had an impact on so many people throughout her short life. She was dedicated to her family (despite feeling trapped as a companion to her mother), the Suffragettes and to the other causes that she took on. While her romantic experiences sadly came to nothing, her experiences in prison highlighted to others the double standards she felt were occurring in the prison systems, something she later highlighted in her book *Prisons and Prisoners*.

Thankfully, her many letters that have been preserved allow the reader to glimpse what sort of kind and dedicated person she was. She spent a lot of time worrying that she had not quite got her point across properly and sometimes her comments came across as rude and abrupt or even condescending. Nonetheless, Con made a huge impact on her family, friends and those that she corresponded with. One hopes that she would have been happy with her life and her achievements, apart from her relationship with John Ponsonby, and it is clear that she would have been terribly pleased her goal of universal suffrage for all women was eventually achieved. Sadly, her persistence to experience the terrible prison conditions for herself hastened her death, not to mention her reliance on the 'scientific' methods of Homer Lane.

Nevertheless, it is hard to disagree with the fact she was an amazing inspiration and martyr to women, leaving us to wonder what she would have made of the world today.

Perhaps the final words should be left to Con's dear friend Maurice Baring, who wrote the following sentiments in *The Letters of Constance Lytton* when it was first published in 1925, two years after her death:

You were a summer's day, all warmth and tune,
Your soul a harbour, dark beneath the moon,
And flashing with soft lights of sympathy.

Biographical Appendix

Herbert Henry Asquith (1852-1928). A liberal politician who served as Prime Minister between 1908 and 1916. During his premiership, female suffrage created much debate between the Liberals. Mr Asquith himself opposed votes for women for most of his career, believing that it would disproportionately benefit the Conservatives. As Prime Minister, he was a target for many militant suffragettes.

Elizabeth (Betty) Balfour (née Bulwer-Lytton) (1867-1942). Educated by governesses during the family's overseas postings, Betty married Gerald Balfour, an ambitious politician, in 1887. The family home, Fishers Hall, in Woking, was designed by Edwin Lutyens, her sister Emily's husband, while Gertrude Jekyll designed the gardens. Betty preferred the suffrage society the CUFWA (Conservative and Unionist Women's Franchise Association), which had close links to the NUWSS (National Union of Women's Suffrage Societies) as opposed to the more militant WSPU. Betty's book *The Letters of Constance Lytton* was published by William Heinemann in 1925 shortly after Con's tragic death. Betty was very active politically herself and was Woking's first female councillor. She was also good friends with the composer and Suffragette Ethel Smyth. Betty died of a perforated duodenal ulcer on 28 March 1942.

Gerald Balfour (1853-1945). The younger brother of Prime Minister Arthur Balfour, he was a Conservative MP and served as the Chief

Secretary for Ireland between 1895 and 1900. He was also interested in parapsychology and, despite being married to Con's sister Betty, had an affair with Winifred Coombe Tenant.

The Blathwayts. Eagle House in Batheaston, near Bath, was the home of Emily Blathwayt and her husband Colonel Linley Blathwayt. The house was used between 1909 and 1912 as a refuge for Suffragettes who had recently been released from prison following hunger strikes. Emily and her daughter became affiliated with the WSPU, but Emily resigned when the organisation took a more militant turn. The Suffragette Arboretum can be found in the grounds of the house.

Henry Noel Brailsford (1852-1928). A prolific left-wing journalist who initially started out as a foreign correspondent. A founding member of the Men's League for Women's Suffrage, he resigned from the *Daily News* in 1909 when the newspaper began supporting the forced feeding of Suffragette prisoners. He wrote a number of books over the years and toured central Europe regularly, contributing to various publications.

Jane Brailsford (1874-1937). Married one of her tutors from the University of Glasgow, Henry Brailsford, but it was not to be a happy marriage. She enjoyed being a member of the WSPU, which she joined in 1909. She was released early from prison and, like Con, believed it was because she was the wife of a well-known journalist. She left the WSPU when the Pethick-Lawrences were ejected from the organisation. She separated from her husband in 1921.

Edith Bulwer-Lytton (née Villiers) (1841-1936). Edith had a twin sister called Elizabeth who married Henry Loch. Edith was unmarried and lived with her mother until she met Robert Bulwer-Lytton when she was 23. Two of her children, Edward and Harry, died as infants. Edith was forced to live off a reduced income after her husband's death and join the royal court.

Edward Bulwer-Lytton (1803-1873). An MP and Secretary of State for the Colonies, he declined the crown of Greece after King Otto abdicated in 1862. He later became the Baron of Knebworth in 1866. He wrote a number of literary works and although is little read today, he coined several phrases including the opening line 'It was a dark and stormy night'. His marriage to Rosina Bulwer-Lytton broke down and he had long suffered from a disease of the ear. Edward was buried, against his wishes, in Westminster Abbey.

Neville Bulwer-Lytton (1879-1951). Neville was born in India to Robert and Edith and was one of Con's younger brothers. He was educated at Eton and moved on to the Ecole des Beaux-Arts in Paris. Neville married Judith Blunt in 1899 and later competed in the 1908 Summer Olympics in London. Neville served on the Western Front in the First World War at the Somme and Amiens. He received the Chevalier of the Legion of Honour from the French government. After divorcing Judith in 1923, he married Rosa Alexandra Fortel the following year. He resided in France until his death in Paris in 1951.

Robert Bulwer-Lytton (1831-1891). After his childhood was plighted by his parents' unhappy relationship, he entered diplomatic service at 18. He married Edith Villiers and had seven children, although not all survived past infancy. Robert served as Viceroy of India between 1876 and 1880 and was then the British Ambassador of France between 1887 and 1891. His Indian tenure was controversial due to his handling of the Great Famine of 1876-1878 and the Second Anglo-Afghan War. He was a protégé of Benjamin Disraeli when it came to domestic affairs and resigned his viceroyalty at the same time Disraeli resigned as Prime Minister. Robert was created Earl of

Lytton in the County of Derby and Viscount of Knebworth. Although he died in Paris and received a state funeral, he was buried at the family mausoleum at Knebworth.

Rosina Bulwer-Lytton (née Wheeler) (1802-1882). Rosina was an Anglo-Irish writer who, over the course of her life, published fourteen novels, a volume of essays and a volume of letters. Her mother was the women's rights advocate Anna Wheeler, one of the first women to speak out about women's rights and equal opportunities. Rosina and Edward Bulwer-Lytton legally separated in 1836 after politics had affected their marriage and her children were removed from her care. Her book, *Cheveley or the Man of Honour,* caricatured her ex-husband. She was detained in a lunatic asylum but was later freed after a public outcry.

Victor Bulwer-Lytton (1876-1947). Victor was born in India and was the eldest surviving son to Robert and Edith. He was educated at Eton before moving on to Trinity College, Cambridge. He joined the Admiralty and later became the Governor of Bengal between 1922 and 1927. In 1902 he married Pamela Chichele-Plowden. Both of his sons predeceased him, and his titles went to his younger brother Neville upon his death.

Emily Wilding Davison (1872-1913). Emily won a bursary to study literature at Royal Holloway College, but after her father died in 1893, she was forced to suspend her studies. Davison became a live-in governess and was able to save money in order to complete her studies in 1901. She joined the WSPU in November 1906 and became an officer and chief steward. By 1909 she was working for the WSPU full time. Sylvia Pankhurst described her as 'one of the most daring and reckless of the militants', and she was arrested, imprisoned and force fed many times. On 4 June 1913 she suffered a fatal injury at the Derby, having been knocked unconscious by the King's horse when she stepped onto the track. She never regained consciousness and died four days later, on 8 June. On 14 June, 5,000 women formed a procession with 50,000 people lining the route for her funeral. Her gravestone at Morpeth bears the WSPU slogan 'Deeds not words'.

Flora Drummond (1878-1949). Flora was born in Manchester and trained to become a postmistress, but was deemed too short at 5'1 (just 1 inch too short), which she felt was discrimination. She joined the WSPU in 1906, becoming a paid organiser. Flora was nicknamed 'The General' as she had a habit of leading the suffrage marches wearing a military style uniform along with an officer's cap and epaulettes, sometimes even riding a horse. She made daring and headline stunts and was imprisoned nine times. In 1914 she was forced to recover on the Isle of Arran after a prison stint. During the First World War she took on public speaking and attempted to persuade union workers not to strike.

Una Dugdale (1879-1975). Una was the daughter of Commander Edward Stratford Dugdale who, along with his wife, was a supporter of the suffrage movement. Una attended Cheltenham Ladies College and then went on to Hanover and Paris, where she studied singing. After hearing Christabel Pankhurst speak in Hyde Park in 1907, she toured the country with Mrs Pankhurst. Una's marriage ceremony to Victor Dierderichs Duval sparked controversy in 1912 when she wanted to omit the word 'obey' from her marriage vows, but was forced to use the word anyhow as otherwise her marriage would have been considered illegal. Her husband set up the Men's Political Union for Women's Enfranchisement. Una brought up two daughters after the First World War and was the co-founder and treasurer of the Suffragette Fellowship, an organisation set up to preserve the memories of the militant Suffragettes.

Maria Teresa Earle (née Villiers) (1836-1925). An older sister of Edith and Elizabeth Villiers, she was a horticulturalist and writer on garden subjects, being known as Mrs C.W. Earle to her readers. She was influenced by Gertrude Jekyll and was encouraged to write by her niece, Con, and they jointly produced *Potpourri from a Surrey Garden*. She lived at Woodlands in Cobham, where Con sometimes stayed.

Herbert Gladstone (1854-1930). A Liberal MP, he was Home Secretary between 1906 and 1908, having been appointed by Sir Henry Campbell-Bannerman. During the course of his political career, he played a part in the Liberal welfare reforms, including the Workmen's Compensation Act of 1906, the Children's Act of 1908 and the Trade Boards Act of 1909.

Dr Mary Gordon (1861-1941). Having graduated from the London School of Medicine for Women in 1890, she worked at the East London Hospital for Children, the Evelina London Children's Hospital and then later had a private practice in Harley Street. While working as a physician she highlighted the topics of the effects of prostitution, sexually transmitted diseases, and alcohol dependence on women. Mary supported the suffragette movement and secretly communicated with the WSPU about conditions in prisons. She then became the first British female prison inspector, enacting several improvements in these settings, including prison work allocation. She wrote *Penal Discipline* in 1922, which advocated prison system reforms and then the biographical novel *Chase of the Wildgoose*, also known as *The Llangollen Ladies*, in 1936 about two ladies called Lady Eleanor Butler and Miss Sarah Ponsonby, who lived life their own way.

Annie Kenney (1879-1953). Annie was the fourth daughter out of a total of twelve children, born in Oldham to a working-class family. She worked part time in a cotton mill from 10 years of age and then full time from the age of 13. She became involved in trade unions before becoming a member of the WSPU in 1905 after hearing Teresa Billington-Craig and Christabel Pankhurst speak in Oldham. She trained in public speaking and became the deputy for the WSPU organisation in 1912. Annie endured forced feeding many times and wanted to highlight the horrors of the Cat and Mouse Act. During the First World War she encouraged the trade unions to support war work. She married James Taylor and moved to Letchworth in 1918, where her son was born in 1921.

Jessie Kenney (1887-1985). The seventh daughter out of a family of twelve, her sister Annie was eight years older. She, too, worked in a cotton mill from the age of 13 and also became involved in the WSPU. Although she did not have the same gift for public speaking as her sister, she was very organised and became the secretary for Emmeline Pethick-Lawrence in 1906. In her role she organised members to interrupt important government meetings and sent deputations. At the WSPU march on 18 June 1910, Jessie Kenney led the procession through London on horseback, along with 'General' Flora Drummond. In 1913, Jessie became ill and went to Switzerland to convalesce. She later trained as a wireless operator and became a stewardess.

Dr Alice Stewart Ker (1853-1943). Dr Ker completed her medical training in Ireland and became the thirteenth woman to be registered as a doctor in Britain. She was a house surgeon at the Children's Hospital in Birmingham and then went on to be a GP in Leeds. In 1907 she joined the WSPU and ran the movement's shop, together with Ada Flatman, raising important substantial funds for the cause. Dr Ker played an active part in propaganda work for the WSPU in

Liverpool, and in 1912 was arrested along with around 200 other women for breaking windows at the Harrods store in London and imprisoned at HMP Holloway. After being released due to ill health, Dr Ker campaigned against forced feeding, stating that the procedure was used as a punishment rather than as medical treatment and that the equipment used was not sterilised adequately. There is some disagreement as to whether Alice Ker was herself force fed. Like Con, she was also a vegetarian.

Homer Lane (1875-1925). Born in Connecticut, he trained as a teacher and then worked with delinquent children before moving to England to found the Little Commonwealth. In 1917, he was accused of sexual assault, which led to the closure of the school in 1918. He then worked as a psychoanalyst before he was accused of misconduct, before being accused of being an alien and forced to leave the country. He died shortly afterwards in Paris.

Emily Lutyens (née Bulwer-Lytton) (1874-1964). Emily was born on Boxing Day in Paris and later became a correspondent of the elderly Norfolk clergyman Whitwell Elwin, a contributor and editor of the *Quarterly Review*. After her father's death she fell in love with Wilfred Scawen Blunt (poet and Arabian horse keeper, thirty-five years her senior) and became a lifelong friend of his daughter, Judith Blunt. In 1897 she married Edwin Landseer Lutyens, a leading architect, and went on to have five children. Emily was interested in women's suffrage but was opposed to the militant tactics, and as such resigned from the WSPU in 1909 when they adopted such ideals. In 1910 she joined the Theosophical Society and became a surrogate parent to Krishnamurti in 1911. She was appointed by Annie Besant as the English representative of the Order of the Star in the East. Emily toured the country lecturing on behalf of theosophy and became a vegetarian. She was devoted to Krishnamurti, which placed a huge strain on her marriage.

Kitty Marion (1871-1944). Born Katherina Maria Schäfer in Germany, she emigrated to London when she was 15 and began performing in the music halls. Kitty joined the WSPU initially selling *Votes for Women* on the streets, but soon took part in the militant activism. Her most notorious act was burning down the Hurst Park Race Grandstand on 18 June 1913, along with Clara Giveen. She was force fed over 200 times during her prison sentences. Kitty left England at the start of the First World War because of anti-German sentiment and went to the United States, where she became a birth control advocate.

Adela Pankhurst (1885-1961). The daughter of Emmeline Pankhurst, Adela worked as a political organiser for the WSPU until she moved to Australia in 1914 following an estrangement from her family.

Christabel Pankhurst (1880-1958). The daughter of Emmeline Pankhurst, Christabel moved to Geneva but returned when her father died to help look after her siblings. She obtained a law degree from the University of Manchester but, as a woman, was not allowed to practise. She was the co-founder of the WSPU along with her mother and took on the role of organising secretary, encouraging the more militant actions of the group. Between 1913 and 1914 she lived in France to avoid imprisonment following the Cat and Mouse Act, but returned to England at the start of the First World War and was immediately imprisoned, as she had feared. She wrote a book on sexually transmitted diseases and moved to California in 1921. She was appointed Dame Commander of the Order of the British Empire in the 1936 New Year Honours.

Emmeline Pankhurst (1858-1928). Born in Manchester, Emmeline was introduced to the women's suffrage movement at the age of 14. She worked as a Poor Law Guardian and in 1903 co-founded the WSPU with her daughter Christabel. She halted the militant actions of the organisation at the start of the First World War and encouraged women to help with the war effort. In 1918 the Representation of the People Act concluded the actions of the WSPU, but Emmeline still maintained an interest in the empowerment of women and enjoyed political campaigning.

Sylvia Pankhurst (1882-1960). Sylvia was born in Manchester and as she grew up became interested in the arts. She attended the Royal College of Arts and intended to pursue a career in this field, but became aware of the lack of equal opportunities for women in this area of work. In 1906 she began working full time for the WSPU designing logos and pamphlets using her artistic skills. Both Sylvia and her sister Adela believed in socialism, whereas Christabel and their mother were pushing for the vote for middle-class women. Both Sylvia and Adela had left the WSPU by 1914, having become estranged from the rest of the family. She founded her own cause, the Suffrage Foundation, and started the newspaper *Women's Dreadnought*. Sylvia was opposed to the war but helped defend poor women who were affected by the conflict and later attended communist meetings in Russia. Sylvia objected to the meaning of marriage and the taking of a man's name, consequently giving birth to a child out of wedlock, after which her mother never spoke to her again. Sylvia spent most of her later years campaigning on the behalf of Ethiopia, where she died in 1960.

Emmeline Pethick-Lawrence (1867-1954). One of thirteen children, Emmeline and Mary Neal co-founded the Esperance Club for girls and women for dressmaking and dance. She also started the Maison Esperance, a dressmaking co-operative with minimum wage, eight-hour days and a holiday scheme. As a socialist, Emmeline was shocked by the levels of poverty she witnessed. In 1900 she developed the hostel at Littlehampton for working girls' holidays, where Con stayed. She married Frederick Lawrence in 1901, with both adapting a joint name. She met Emmeline Pankhurst in 1906 and became treasurer of the WSPU, for which she raised £134,000 in six years. Their home became the office of the WSPU and in 1907 she founded *Votes for Women* with her husband. Both her and Frederick were arrested and imprisoned in 1912 for conspiracy to window smash, even though they both disagreed with the act. They were subsequently ousted from the WSPU by Emmeline and Christabel Pankhurst because of a disagreement over the change to militant activism. She subsequently joined the United Suffragists.

John Ponsonby (1866-1952). The son of Sir Henry Ponsonby, Queen Victoria's Private Secretary, John Ponsonby was educated at Eton College and then commissioned into the Coldstream Guards in 1888. He served in Uganda in 1898, the second Boer War in 1900, and was then attached to the Rhodesian Field Force and sent to South Africa in February 1902. He had an on/off love affair with Con, but her family were not keen on her marrying someone of a lower rank, although Con believed it was because he had a hare lip and cleft palate.

Olive Schreiner (1855-1920). An author and campaigner, Olive lived in South Africa and was an advocate for various African groups. She is best known for her novel *The Story of an African Farm*. The website www.oliveschriner.org is a collection and database of over 5,000 letters written to and by Olive, including those to Con, and covers a diverse range of topics.

Ethel Smyth (1858-1944). Ethel was born in Sidcup, Kent, and was the fourth of eight children. She studied music despite her father's opposition. In 1910 she joined the WSPU, giving up music for two years so that she could devote herself to the cause. Her 'March of the Women' became the anthem of the women's suffrage movement. Ethel served two months in Holloway prison for stone throwing.

She had a number of romantic affairs, many with women. Ethel was recognised as a composer and was made a Dame Commander of the Order of the British Empire in 1922, and also received honorary doctorates in music from the universities of Oxford and Durham.

Georgina Solomon (1844-1933). A British campaigner and educator, Georgina and her daughter, Daisy, joined the WSPU in 1908 after her Liberal politician husband passed away. She was imprisoned for breaking nine windows of the Black Rod Office in the House of Lords on 4 March 1912. She left the WSPU in 1913 but remained active in other suffrage organisations, as well as other movements designed to improve social purity.

Marie Stopes (1880-1958). Marie was born in Scotland but soon moved to London. She studied botany and geology at university and became the youngest person to receive a doctorate of science. Her hugely successful *Married Love* was published in 1918. She then wrote a book on birth control and opened a mothers' clinic in Holloway in 1921. She gradually built up a small network of clinics across Britain, which are now part of the Marie Stopes International Organisation. Also known for her controversial views on eugenics and racial superiority, she bought a lighthouse on the Isle of Portland in Dorset to escape the trials of London and founded and curated a local museum. She died of breast cancer in 1958.

Adela Smith (née Villiers) (1872-1956). Adela was Con's cousin and lifetime correspondent. She married the British MP Sir Francis Smith on 27 July 1901 and had one child, Stephen Francis Villiers-Smith. Adela suffered several periods of ill health, including tuberculosis, and Con would often help look after her. Olive Schreiner met Adela and her cousin Con during a visit to their aunt, Lady Loch, and her husband Henry Loch at the Cape and they became good friends.

Bibliography

Archives

The British Library
Hertfordshire Archives
Knebworth House Archives
Museum of London
The Women's Library, LSE

Books and Journal Articles

Atkinson, Diane, *Rise up Women!* (Bloomsbury, London 2018)
Balfour, Betty, *Letters of Constance Lytton* (William Heinemann, London 1925)
Bryant, Violet, 'The Treatment of Political Prisoners' in *Votes for Women*, 4 February 1910
Bull Templar Strangways, Henry, 'An Ex-Premier's Sympathy' [letter], *Votes for Women*, 8 October 1909
Colmore, G. and Lee, A., *Suffragette Sally* (Broadview Press, 2008)
Curtis, Mavis, *What the Suffragists Did Next* (Amberley, Stroud 2017)
Lytton, Constance, *Prisons and Prisoners: some personal experiences* (William Heinemann, London 1914)
Maud, C., *No Surrender* (Persephone Books, London 2011)
Mulvey-Roberts, Marie, *The Militants: Suffragette Activism* (Routledge/Thoemmes Press, London 1994)

Mulvey-Roberts, Marie, 'Militancy, Masochism or Martyrdom? The Public and Private Prisons of Constance Lytton', in Sandra Holton and June Purvis (eds.) *Votes for Women* (Routledge, London 2000)

Pankhurst, E., *The Importance of the Vote* (The Woman's Press, London 1908)

Philips, Melanie, *The Ascent of Woman* (Abacus, St Ives 2003)

Robinson, Jane, *Hearts and Minds* (Doubleday, London 2018)

Schreiner, Olive, *Woman and Labour* (Virago, London 1978)

Smyth, E., *Female Pipings in Eden* (P. Davies, London 1934)

Tickner, Lisa, *The Spectacle of Women: Imagery of the Suffrage Campaign 1907-14* (Chatto & Windus, London 1987)

Thomas, S., 'Scenes in the writing of "Constance Lytton and Jane Warton, spinster": contextualising a cross-class dresser', *Women's History Review*, 12(1)

Vicinus, Martha, *Independent Women: Work and Community for Single Women 1850-1920* (Virago, London 1985)

Wright, Almroth, *The Unexpurgated Case Against Woman Suffrage* (Constable, London 1913)

Newspapers

Daily Mail
Dundee Courier
The Times
Votes for Women

Index

Asquith, Herbert 56, 57, 68, 74, 75, 78, 84, 85, 91, 100, 111, 118, 120, 122, 134, 168
Aunt T *see* Earle, Mrs Charles
Austria 3, 4, 68, 69, 70

Balfour, Arthur 4, 65, 68, 75, 76, 117, 118-9, 164, 168
Balfour, Betty *see* Bulwer-Lytton, Betty
Balfour, Frances 4, 42
Balfour, Gerald 3, 4, 11, 20, 23, 45. 73-4, 75, 76, 164, 165, 168-9
Baring, Maurice 21, 29, 30, 31, 32-3, 34, 69, 162, 163, 167
Bennett, Curtis 46, 49, 50
Birmingham 73, 75, 76, 77, 81, 114, 174
birth control 3, 146, 151, 152, 176, 179
Blackshaw, George 152
Blathwayt 74, 116, 169
Bloomfield, Lady 7, 33, 34, 37
Bloomsbury Square 97, 128
Blunt, Judith *see* Bulwer-Lytton, Judith
Bow Street 46, 47, 49, 51, 56, 57, 121
Brailsford, Henry 83, 99, 169
Brailsford, Jane 76, 78, 79, 81, 86, 99, 169
Bryant, Violet 78, 86, 180
Bulwer-Lytton, Betty 1, 3-4, 5, 11-12, 13, 14, 20-1, 23, 26, 27, 30, 31, 34, 35, 38, 42, 45, 52, 53, 61, 63, 64, 65, 66, 67, 68, 95, 111, 115, 117, 118, 127, 142, 145, 151, 153, 156, 157, 158, 159, 162, 164, 165, 168, 169, 180
Bulwer-Lytton, Edith 1, 5, 11, 16, 17, 18, 19, 20, 21, 22, 26-7, 28-9, 32, 33, 52, 53, 65, 75, 81, 108, 140, 153-5, 157, 158-9, 162, 165, 166, 169-70, 171, 173
Bulwer-Lytton, Edward 1, 2, 84, 170, 171

Bulwer-Lytton, Emily 3, 4, 16, 20, 21, 25, 34, 42, 64, 68, 91, 95, 97, 98, 99, 128, 129, 147, 149, 153, 155, 165, 168, 175

Bulwer-Lytton, Judith 29, 52, 170, 175

Bulwer-Lytton, Neville 3, 11, 12, 29, 33, 34, 37, 52, 109, 153, 158, 161, 170, 171

Bulwer-Lytton, Pamela 27-8, 29, 30, 32-3, 109, 157, 158, 171

Bulwer-Lytton, Robert 1, 2-3, 5, 13, 147, 161, 169, 170-1

Bulwer-Lytton, Rosina 1, 2, 170, 171

Bulwer-Lytton, Victor 3, 8, 9, 10, 12, 19, 24, 25, 27, 28, 30, 32, 33, 34, 64, 66, 68, 73, 75, 98, 99-100, 101-102, 108, 109, 115, 133, 150, 151, 153-5, 156, 157, 158, 159, 160, 171

Campbell-Bannerman, Henry 35, 173

Cape Town 9

Cat and Mouse Act, The 134-5, 174, 176

Cavell, Edith 141

Caxton Hall 43, 55

church 8-9, 12, 22, 37, 59, 111, 160

Churchill, Winston 29, 102, 107

Clements Inn 43, 47, 50, 54, 91, 109

cookbook 154, 155

Conciliation Bill 99, 100, 108, 109, 111, 119, 120

Conservative and Unionist Women's Suffrage Association 42, 65, 111, 168

Coombe Tennant JP, Mrs Winifred 112, 131, 162, 169

court 44, 46, 48, 49, 50, 56, 57, 77, 121

Daily Mail, The 36, 53, 142, 146, 181

Daily News, The 69, 117, 169

Danes, The 13, 22, 25

Davison, Emily Wilding 76, 77, 79, 88, 131, 171

deputations 35, 36, 43, 47, 55, 64, 68, 70, 71, 72, 76, 100, 120, 122, 126, 127, 140, 162, 174

Disraeli, Benjamin 1

doctors 58-9, 60, 61, 74, 81, 86, 89-90, 93-4, 95-6, 97, 98-9, 102, 104-105, 106, 107, 113, 114, 124, 125, 134, 137, 146, 158, 174

Dogs 3, 10, 12, 32, 141
Drummond, Flora 46, 48, 51, 84, 172, 174
Dugdale, Una 56, 57, 125, 172
Dundee Courier, The 56, 81, 84, 181
Dunlop, Marion Wallace 47, 105

Earl of Lytton, The 3, 13, 99, 101, 147, 155
Earle, Mrs Charles 4, 13, 15, 18-19, 22, 23, 24, 25, 26, 27, 28, 29, 30, 31, 32, 34, 36, 52-3, 54, 64, 67, 72, 108, 129, 140, 151, 162, 173
Esperance Club, The 37, 177
Euston Road 108, 121, 128

Fahey, Caprina 55, 56
Fawcett, Mrs Henry (Millicent) 35, 109, 142
Florence 21, 29
flower arranging 4, 21, 141, 166
forced feeding 81, 85, 86, 87, 89-90, 103, 104, 105, 113, 114, 121, 124, 125, 129, 133, 139, 148, 169, 174, 175

Fraülein Oser 3, 5, 97
funeral 160-1

Gawthorpe, Mary 85, 92, 108
George, David Lloyd 76, 77, 78, 119-20
Gladstone, Herbert 43, 47, 48-9, 68, 74, 83, 102, 105, 173
Gordon, Dr Mary 40, 108, 133, 143, 151, 153, 173
Grey, Edward Sir 67, 118

Hall, Leslie 86, 115
Heart 21, 60, 86, 89, 92, 94, 96, 99, 101, 105, 113, 129
disease 32, 77-8, 83, 90, 98, 102, 114, 117, 121, 122, 124, 128, 130, 133, 151, 156, 161, 165
Holloway 35, 38, 40, 44, 51, 57-62, 70, 73, 84, 94, 103, 106-107, 121, 134, 135-7, 145, 147, 175, 178, 179
Home Office, the 47, 74, 90-1, 96, 98, 102, 103, 106, 115, 134, 149, 160
Home Secretary, the 43, 45, 48-9, 74, 77-8, 83, 94, 98, 101, 102, 104, 70, 105, 113-14, 173

Homewood 18, 27, 28-9, 32, 54, 68, 75, 108, 130, 141, 142, 145, 151, 153, 154, 155-6, 157
hospital 51, 58, 61, 65, 99, 142, 173, 174
House of Commons, the 46, 48, 55, 66, 70, 83, 91, 98, 162
Howey, Elsie 74, 79
hunger strikes 77, 80, 82, 83, 90, 91, 98, 101, 105, 113, 129, 138, 145, 169

India 3, 11, 14-5, 97, 154, 156, 158, 160, 170

JP *see* Ponsonby, John
journalism 8, 12, 14-6, 21, 26

Kenney, Annie 38, 39, 40, 42, 43, 67, 74, 76, 84, 87, 100, 107, 109, 116, 118, 140, 145, 149, 150, 174
Kenney, Jessie 38, 74,149, 174
Ker, Dr Alice 87, 106, 128, 136, 174-5
Kirkpatrick Watts, Ellen 56, 57
Knebworth vi, 3, 5, 7, 8, 11, 13, 25, 28, 37, 67, 95, 108, 152, 160-1, 162, 171, 180
Krishnamurti 155, 175

lady in waiting 22, 27, 31
Lane, Homer 148-51, 153, 154, 155-7, 158, 159, 160, 167, 175
Lansbury, George 138-9
Lawless, Leslie 121-2
Lawson, Leslie 56, 57
Leigh, Mary 76-7, 114
Letters of Constance Lytton, The 1, 11, 23, 35, 52, 53, 127, 162, 167, 168, 180
Little Commonwealth 141, 148-9, 150, 156, 175
Littlehampton 37, 39, 40, 42, 45, 177
Liverpool 73, 76, 81, 82, 90, 91, 95-6, 97, 98, 99, 100, 102, 106, 113-14, 115, 123, 124, 175
Loch(s) 9, 10, 54, 169, 179
Lord, Daisy 62
Lucile 1
Lutyens, Edwin 25, 28, 168, 175
Lutyens, Emily *see* Bulwer-Lytton, Emily

MacDonald, Meredith 65, 73
magistrates 46, 47, 48, 49, 56, 57, 78, 86, 89, 90, 94, 122
Manchester 35, 43, 78, 81, 85, 88, 114, 118, 172, 176, 177

Mansel, Mildred 84, 97, 116
Marion, Kitty 78, 83, 131, 176
Married Love 145, 146, 147, 179
Marsh, Edward 29, 107
Martin, Selena 85-6, 115
Memories of a Militant 39, 42
Meredith, Owen 1
Morris dancing 37
Mother's Clinic 145-6
mutilation 60-1

National Review 9, 15, 67
Neal, Mary 37, 177
Newcastle 76, 77, 78, 79, 80, 81, 86, 92, 94, 98, 99, 101, 114
Nield, Herbert 44, 45

organisers 79, 83, 88, 108, 116, 172, 176

National Union of Women's Suffrage Societies (NUWSS) 35, 65, 109, 168

Pankhurst, Adela 83, 84, 116, 176, 177
Pankhurst, Christabel 35, 44, 46, 48, 51, 57, 75, 76, 77, 87, 92, 95, 106, 108, 118, 125, 145, 172, 174, 176, 177, 178

Pankhurst, Emmeline 45, 46, 48, 49, 50, 51, 54, 68-9, 72, 75, 82, 84, 87, 106, 107, 116, 126, 137, 140-1, 150, 172, 176, 178
Pankhurst, Sylvia 51, 55, 123, 132, 171, 177
Paris 2, 4, 5, 13, 151, 160, 170, 171, 172, 175
parliament 46, 47, 48, 49, 55, 56, 78, 80, 83, 91, 111, 116, 119, 120, 126, 133, 142
Peace, Rachel 134, 148
Pethick-Lawrence, Emmeline 37, 40, 47, 50, 51, 55, 56, 64, 67, 68, 87, 103, 108, 123, 125, 129, 146, 150
Pethick-Lawrence, Frederick 42, 43, 177, 178
piano playing 3, 16
Plowden, Pamela *see* Bulwer-Lytton, Pamela
Ponsonby, John 10-11, 14, 17-21, 23, 28, 29, 30, 33, 34, 41, 150, 153, 156-7, 163, 165, 167, 178
Ponsonby, Lady 14, 21
Ponsonby, Maggie 14, 21, 157
Potpourri from a Surrey Garden 24, 25-6, 173
prison governor 88, 89, 90, 94, 96-7, 103, 124

prison reformation 2, 3, 26, 28, 29, 38, 39, 41, 45, 62, 63, 107, 109, 129, 131, 143, 156, 162, 166, 173
Prisons and Prisoners vii, 3, 28, 38, 40, 41, 47, 63, 66, 68, 77, 87, 90, 100, 122-4, 125, 131-2, 133, 139, 142, 164, 167, 180
psychoanalysis 148, 149

Queen Alexandra 26-7, 31
Queen's Hall 46, 51, 81, 97, 98, 112, 146
Queen Victoria 2, 7, 10, 11, 22, 26, 155, 178

Realm, The 15
Representation of the People Act 142, 177
rheumatism 5, 21, 22, 27, 28, 144
Ruggles-Brise, Sir Evelyn 40, 109
Rule 243A 102-103

Schreiner, Olive 10, 11, 23-4, 34, 40, 54, 124, 128, 130, 131-2, 140, 144, 145, 178, 179, 181
second division 44, 45, 48, 60, 77

Selborne, Lady 117
Smith, Mrs Francis *see* Villiers, Adela
Smyth, Ethel 43, 105, 109, 133, 135, 138, 168, 178-9, 181
Solomon, Daisy 55, 57, 135, 179
Stopes, Marie 145-8, 152, 166, 179
stroke 127-8, 129, 130, 133, 143, 145, 150, 166

Tavistock Square 156, 157
third division 44, 45, 88, 103
Times, The 69, 72, 78, 81, 83, 102, 115, 117, 133, 146, 181
Troup, Edward 102, 115

vegetarianism 18, 28, 33, 115, 175
Viceroy of India 2, 3, 5, 13, 14-5, 160, 170
Vienna 2
Villiers, Adela 4, 7, 9, 11, 17, 22-3, 25, 29, 32, 38, 39, 53, 81, 130-1, 140, 141, 144, 179
Villiers, Edith *see* Bulwer-Lytton, Edith
Votes for Women (newspaper) 40, 43, 68, 79, 80, 85, 86, 95, 98, 100, 105, 107, 109, 114, 119, 123, 128, 137, 176, 178, 180, 181

Walton prison 85-6, 88-91, 96-7, 102, 112, 114, 124, 130
Warton, Jane 2, 42, 85-111, 113, 115, 123, 125, 128, 130, 136, 166, 181
Westminster 28, 43, 56, 112, 121, 170
Wheeler, Anna 1, 171
window smashing 61, 77, 78, 79, 85, 94, 121, 126-7, 129, 174, 177, 179

Women's Dreadnought, The 133, 161-2, 177
Woodlands 23, 27, 29, 32, 34, 173
Women's Social and Political Union (WSPU) 35, 36, 37, 40, 41, 42-3, 45, 46-7, 51, 55, 56, 61, 72, 74, 76, 83, 84, 85, 86, 88, 91, 99-100, 101, 106, 108, 109-10, 111, 112, 116, 119, 120, 127, 132, 143, 150, 157, 168, 169, 171-2, 173, 174, 175, 176-9